God, You Must Think I'm Crazy

EMI LYNN

ISBN 978-1-63575-485-8 (Paperback)
ISBN 978-1-63575-486-5 (Digital)

Christian Faith Publishing, Inc.
296 Chestnut Street
Meadville, PA 16335
www.christianfaithpublishing.com

Printed in the United States of America

Contents

Foreword

This manuscript covers more than forty years of seeking God with a few steps forward and then interludes of many steps backward. Feelings of failure run rampant but the genuine heartfelt search for God's will is always there. It is the author's sincere desire that relaying these honest encounters and real emotions will help at least one person in their quest of pleasing and serving God.

The Old Trailer

The trailer was old, manufactured in 1956, but a well-made one in its day. The year was 1996 and the coldest January that I can remember before or since. I had been moving in for about a week. The trailer home was without heat but since we have pretty mild winters in the Gulf Coast area, I was not worried. My younger brother had already been asked to pick up a window unit that was combination air and heat and install it for me. During the week that I was moving in, even though my son had replaced quite a bit of the flooring in the hall and living room and had done a lot of painting and cosmetic repairs, it was discovered that the entire floor underneath the cabinets in the kitchen was rotted. A friend volunteered his son to tear it out (With pay!). He was supposed to replace it but as young people are prone to do, he quit. It was already freezing that day and I was planning on staying my first night, so I was pleading with him to finish. His solution was to stuff the huge hole with newspaper and leave to get ready for his date. I had a small electric heater by my bed but when I arose at about 5:00 a.m. the next morning and started down the hall praying, the cold air from that part of the trailer house hit full force. Just as I raised my hands in the air thanking God for everything that I felt was coming my way, peace, joy, happiness, etc., the ridiculousness of my situation hit me and suddenly I blurted out, *"God, you must think I'm crazy."* My Father and I had a good laugh after that.

The Beginning (Sort Of)

Peterinarians Writers and Missionaries
Does God Really Grow Money
There Was a Bunch of Them
Growing into Adulthood

The beginning of my life was pretty noneventful. The first, and only child for nine years, of working class parents whose love was never doubted by me and is probably the reason that I have been able to accept the unconditional love of my Heavenly Father. My earliest memories are of going to Sunday school and church and memorizing verses of scripture mixed in with my fervent endeavors to teach all of my little friends how to be saved which included trying to put the fear of eternal hell into their little souls.

Peterinarians Writers and Missionaries

My granddaughter announced that she would be a "Peterinarian." She is only in the first grade so of course we didn't have the heart to correct her because it was so cute. I pray that God will grant her the desires of her heart and she will not only be what she wants to be but will be used in his kingdom. As humans, we so easily stray and get side tracked. I still remember what I told my teacher, "a missionary and a writer." My teacher had written some complimentary notes on a little story that I had written, so I know where half of it came from but I'm not sure why I said missionary. I certainly wasn't encouraged in that type of service at home and I'm not sure how I understood the concept as I knew no one personally that served God in the mission field. I kept that desire in my heart until I was married and still pondered over it for years. Could it be that God had a plan for me that I did not fulfill?

Prov. 8:17 King James Version, " I love them that love me; and those that seek me early shall find me."

Does God Really Grow Money

I didn't get the expected reaction from my dad. He just looked at me like, well… like I was *crazy* and said, "Do you expect me to believe that God grows money in drawers." I didn't know what I believed about that but I did know that my God could do anything he wanted.

I had been taught about tithing at a very young age. Consequently, I gave ten cents out of every dollar I was given. When I was about thirteen or fourteen years of age, I became an entrepreneur by paying my mom fifteen cents for a sack lunch each day out of the money my Dad gave me each week for lunches at the school cafeteria. Since lunches were thirty cents and he allowed me fifty cents a day, I made a nifty little profit. No matter how much I explained it, my friends could not believe I paid my mother for lunch. I negotiated with my dad for additional allowance money, so with payment for extra chores, my lunch money, and the free gratis allowance, I netted about $5.00 a week. I had a habit of throwing my money in one of my dresser drawers. When I needed it I just reached in and took out a dollar or two. I don't remember any sacrifices. I always took some for the soda fountain when I went to the grocery store with my parents on Friday night. I went to the movies on Saturday with my friends if I wanted to. I had long since quit calculating a tenth of what I had. I just reached in that drawer every Sunday and took some out for my offering. I was in the junior department and one Sunday, the head teacher of the class announced that I had given the largest offering that year and presented me with a plaque that my mother still had displayed when she left earth to meet our Heavenly Father (I'm sure they must have been teaching about tithing.). I don't remember the total but I *do remember* that the calculator in my mind was working. I should have no money in that dresser drawer! When I returned home, I immediately went to my stash and dollar bills were plentiful. I counted it for the first time since I had been putting it in there. I summoned my dad. I reasoned that he should be even more in awe of the miracle than I was. After all, it was he who had taught me the joy of tithing and I had just taken it a step further with giving but no matter what he thought, I know that my God didn't think I was crazy at all that day. Luke 6:38, "Give, and it shall be given unto you; good measure, pressed down, and shaken together, and running over, shall men give unto your bosom. For with the same measure that ye mete withal, it shall be measured to you again."

There Was a Bunch of Them

The family that lived across the street had five children. Being an only child until age nine, the three oldest were at our house all the time which was great for me. The oldest, a boy, was a year older but we were the best of friends and played cowboys and climbed trees together. The next, a girl, was my age who went just about everywhere with us, even on vacation. She wasn't my best friend but she was so easy going and never openly disagreed with me, thus my parents' choice. The third child, a girl, was a year younger and was someone to be bossed around. The family was totally unchurched. Until they moved away, when I was about fourteen, they became a mission for me. All of them went to Sunday school from time to time with my family (which by my eleventh birthday included two little brothers) especially the girl that was my age. Once, I even persuaded their father to go to church. I rode back with them and all the way, he teased me and asked questions such as "How do you know there is a God." My last big push was right before they moved. An uncle came from up north to visit. He was there quite a while and when he told me he couldn't go to church because he didn't have a white shirt, I went home to get one of my dad's shirts. I was surprised that my dad was not happy about it and said he would probably never get it back (he was right). The target of my evangelistic efforts did go to church but that was it. These people were incorrigible as far as I was concerned. I had some contact with the family as a young adult and tracked one of them down again about ten years later. Then I lost all contact with them. A few years and moves later, I had a chance encounter with the oldest boy and found that his dad had become a Christian as well as himself. Two sisters were actively serving God in other states and two family members were missionaries including my friend's husband, and her son was a youth pastor in a church not far from me. I was so elated.

I may have given up on them but God didn't.

Isa. 55:11, "So shall my word be that goeth forth out of my mouth: it shall not return unto me void, but it shall accomplish that which I please, and it shall prosper in the thing whereto I sent it." The word is true *even* if the messenger *is* a little crazy.

A Young Adult

My years in junior high and high school were happy and contented. I had always felt God's love and loved him back. Then when I was fourteen, I repented and asked God into my heart. At that age there is really nothing to name for forgiveness except admitting that you are, as all mankind, a sinner. I can only imagine the great peace that comes into someone's heart who has truly been away from God because I felt an immediate difference when the Holy Spirit of God filled my soul. I didn't know that I could even love him more and have more of a desire to serve him. In the meantime, I had good friends that were actually "good." We stayed out of trouble and most of our little "gang" had high morals and lofty spiritual goals. I made good grades and won academic awards. I was elected to several offices in school and won a couple of popularity titles. I had my own article with a "by line" for the school newspaper and was junior editor of the yearbook. Life was good and I aspired to write a book complete with my own illustrations, marry a missionary and move with him to a foreign land, and at the very least work for a newspaper as a writer. It didn't happen. I got a job, got married, inherited a family and added to it the very first year by having a son. Now I had three daughters and two sons.

The following years were busy and spiritually unproductive. The burning desire that I had in my soul gradually waned; and although I still attended church and prayed, I felt empty. I began searching again, in earnest, for God's will.

Hearing from Heaven

The Light of Timothy
That "Spittin Up"
Grandpa's Lightning

The Light of Timothy

All of a sudden, what looked like a penlight, lit up one scripture. I was the only one awake in the house so it was with somewhat of an alarm that I turned around to see who might be behind me with a light. There was no one, but the light was definitely over one verse, 2 Timothy 3:5, "Having a form of godliness, but denying the power thereof." I had begun a search to get closer to God after feeling a void in my busy life. Shortly after, I was invited to a revival of a different denomination. I was so touched by the seemingly super spiritual congregation. The visiting evangelist came and sat right in front of my husband and me. I don't remember the rest of the conversation but I do remember asking him a question about what he believed concerning the Holy Spirit and how he works in our lives today. I expected him to pull out his Bible and start showing me scriptures to support his belief. I was used to the art of debating the word to prove that you were right. Instead, he looked at me and with a kind and sincere voice, he said, "Why don't you read the book of Acts, and make sure you ask God to direct you and lead you to the truth." I was astounded, this pastor was going to let me walk out, knowing he might never see me again, without trying to prove his point. All I could think of was that he actually trusted *me* to let God direct me. But, as I look back, his trust was not in me but in a *God* that would not fail me. I decided to read one of the Gospels and then the rest of the New Testament. I was teaching Sunday school at the time, and as I read and prayed, the thought of leaving the church that I grew up in and then uprooting my family as well, seemed unthinkable. The book of Acts was revealed to me in a new way but I was determined to keep reading with the thought in the back of my mind that I would feel vindicated to stay right where I was. It was after about four days of reading that I came to the verse in Timothy. I could not deny it any longer, that it was me denying the power. I finished reading the rest of the books but it was with a different conviction and different heart. Oh God, please let us always be open to you and your will for our lives.

That "Spittin Up"

I was pregnant and suffering from a bad case of acid reflux. Having been diagnosed with stomach ulcers at age sixteen with the diagnosis that these ulcers had been with me since birth, I learned how to eat and how to fend off attacks. The prognosis given by my doctors had not been positive. The largest ulcer had healed after treatment and left in its place, a large scar. I was told the condition would never be cured, only healed, and could easily be irritated and form another ulcer. It was revealed through extensive testing that there were numerous old scars, some of which had been with me since an infant and would, as the doctors said, "always be with me." The medical advice I was given was to eat foods that would not irritate or inflame my stomach in any way and to take medication for relaxing the stomach muscles before eating. Then there was my own solution, keep Pepto-Bismol in abundance, in the house, at my mother's house and in the car, readily available to guzzle down when needed while asking God to forgive me for eating those potato chips on an empty stomach. Now, nothing was working with the acid reflux that had plagued me for most of my pregnancy. My doctor prescribed a medication that reminded me of Alka-Seltzer that helped some, but I still slept upright on the couch to avoid the many times I felt that I had almost choked to death while still half asleep. I was in my sixth month and it had become almost unbearable. I was avoiding food, taking my medicine, and still being awakened all through the night gagging. One night, I threw up my medicine, took it for the second time and went back to sleep only to wake up choking and spitting the medicine back up again. After the third time, I was in the bathroom hanging over the tub with green acid coming out of, not only my mouth, but my nose. I knew that my life could come to an abrupt end if I couldn't breathe and the acid burned my nostrils like I was on fire. I cried out "God, you have to do something or I'm going to die." I feel like I cried out audibly but even if it was in my mind, it was *loud*. Instantly the discharge from my mouth and nose stopped as did the burning. Even now, when I think of it, it seems unbelievable. I thought, "Wow, God just delivered me from this torment." I went back to the couch and sat down in my usual position, stacked my pillows on both sides of me to keep me from lying down when I fell asleep thus helping to prevent strangulation. I awoke the next morning, having slept soundly the rest of the night, and found myself lying flat on the couch with not even a pillow under my head. All of the pillows were on the floor. I went about my day not mentioning anything because, after all, what if I said something about God's goodness and then I became sick that night. *I certainly didn't want to embarrass Almighty God.* The second night I took my position on the couch with my pillows and woke up the next morning the exact same way as I had the morning before. Not only that, I had forgotten to take my medicine. I hate to admit it but I know if I *had* thought of it, I would have taken it. I still didn't say anything, but the third night I climbed into bed with my husband as he tried to discourage me from doing so (he had seen all he wanted to from earlier nights). I said, "I *think* God has healed me from that 'spittin up.'" That was the pet name for my condition. He was a little reluctant; but after a peaceful night, he proclaimed my healing the next morning which was a Wednesday. I still kept quiet. That night we went to church, and as we walked in, some close friends joined us. As my husband gestured toward me, he exclaimed, "God has healed her of that spittin up." They smiled and asked me if it was indeed so.

My answer, "I *guess* so." That night, while praying around the altar, I became jealous of the blessings my husband was seemingly receiving. After all, I was the good person and had always been righteous, but not so with him. I became despondent and was pouting like a spoiled child. No one knew the condition of my heart but my Savior and I. I went to sleep that night feeling very hurt and down. During the night, I awoke and felt liquid coming out of my nose and mouth. I cupped my hands under my chin and ran to the bathroom. Silently, I hung over the bath tub as I realized that a steady stream was pouring down. It was coming from my nose. It was coming out of my mouth. I was not choking or gagging. It was green but I was not burning at all. The message of this situation became clear as I asked for another chance. What a gentle reminder of what he had done for me. The rest of my pregnancy was totally symptom free and I didn't take another drop of medicine. Whether we are *spoiled brats* or a little *crazy*, he loves us with an everlasting love.

Rom. 8:35, "Who shall separate us from the love of Christ? Shall tribulation, or distress."

Grandpa's Lightning

I was just a little girl when I heard my grandpa tell his story about the lightning that struck him in the barn. Everyone in the family called themselves Baptist at the time, although my dad told me there was no regular church attendance when they were young. From time to time a traveling evangelist would come through with his tent and that was when they had organized worship. I don't know how many family members were in the room when he began his story, but I'm sure that I was just an eavesdropper in an adult conversation. I'm not sure now what his exact words were, but this is what I heard. My grandpa was out in the barn praying for some time when lightning came into that barn and struck him. He was out on the ground for hours before he came to. It was an exciting story for me as I pictured in my mind the lightning that came from the sky to zap my grandpa. I was sure he was lucky to be alive. Later, as I grew older and wiser, I wondered about this story and grew to believe that the teller had relished in entertaining his audience so much that the story was stretched somewhat. But then again, I reasoned, maybe it was true and God healed him and saved him from his terrible misfortune because he had been praying for so long. Soon the memory was stored in the files of my computer brain only to be pulled up later when it was triggered by an event that happened to me. It was a Sunday night service and had gone long. I was tired and ready to get my children home when my oldest daughter, who was about twelve years of age at the time, decided to pray at the altar. I would like to say I was in a spiritual frame of mind and in tune with God as I stood by her and dutifully held my left hand under her right elbow to give her support, but the only thing I was feeling *was tired*. If you've never prayed for an extended time with your arms lifted up high in the air, then you may not know how tired your arms can get but I, as her mother, felt I needed to be her support. As our young assistant pastor walked toward us, I was looking at him as he reached over to lay hands on my daughter. Her elbow was lightly resting on my hand as he touched her forehead and in that instant I felt an electric shock that seemed to be transmitted from her arm to my hand and then my whole body. My last memory before I hit the floor, flat on my back, was the pastor's hand and the electric shock that hit me. Could this be the lightning that my grandpa felt? It must have been and I'm sure he knew it! I was eleven when he died. Oh, how I wish I could talk to him about that experience.

The Sad and Painful Years

Timothy
I Desire Your Praises
There Are Roses in the Garden
I Still Love You
Genesis 38
Mark and Mary Became Mark
Have Thine Own Way, Lord. Or Do You

Timothy

The day I brought Timothy home from the hospital was uneventful other than I felt such a peace and happiness. Unlike my first delivery with his older brother, I had breezed through with minimal pain and no lasting unpleasant symptoms. I enjoyed him tremendously and sat for long periods of time allowing him to sleep as I held him. Actually, every time I tried to put him down in his bed, he woke up and cried so I held him for his naps much of the time. I was very protective of him and when he attempted to climb on a chair or something similar, I was right behind him. He spent a lot of time in his little walker racing through the house. I had plenty of help with his older brothers and sisters and he did a lot in his short little life. There were picnics and just trips to the park with no picnic. We all adored him and he never lacked for attention. One day when he was just a few months old and asleep in his bed, I walked in from doing house hold chores. As I stood there just looking at him with a heart full of love and gratitude, I lifted my arms in the air and started to thank my Father for this wonderful gift. Instead of what I intended to say, I blurted out "Not Timothy." I didn't know what had happened. I was feeling happy and grateful with absolutely no fear and yet these words came out in a troubled and pleading way. Then I immediately went back to my feelings from the minute before and began praising God and thanking him for my precious baby. Although this troubled me, I soon put it in the back of my mind and went on. The days that followed were routine and happy. Then the unthinkable tragedy happened. On a Sunday afternoon, the young man next door to us ran over him in the driveway with all of the children right there in the yard. He was a week away from fourteen months old. The Friday before, he stayed with my mother for the first time and when we picked him up on Saturday, she commented on how sweet he had been and how much she had enjoyed him. In the past, he had cried too much to leave him. We left her house and stopped at the grocery store. I jumped out to run in and pick up some milk and as usual intended to leave him in the car with the older children. He protested so much that the kids were saying "just take him" so I did. As I was checking out, with him in one arm and the milk in the other, he started slobbering all over me and giving me so much sugar that the checker commented on how much he loved his mama, to which I replied, "this is unusual, he is usually very stingy with his kisses." The next morning at church, I had another surprise. The sweet lady in the nursery was so shocked as he went to her willingly. She was very distraught at the funeral and kept saying, "He was so sweet Sunday morning." That day in church my good and longtime friend who had consistently tried to make friends with him and hold him to no avail was in front of us with him sitting on my lap. Suddenly he took off his shoe and threw it at her head. Of course she turned around and I motioned that it was him and as she laughed and said, "You little devil," he reached for her. She held him the rest of the time and smothered him with love… then he was gone and I am crying now.

I Desire Your Praises

I couldn't believe it. Yet it was true. The Lord of the universe had broken through the veil of the natural and spoken those words to *me*. It had been eight days since the funeral, and the special services that I had been attending every night at my home church had ended. As the evening drew near that day, I felt that I could not make it without being in the presence of God one more time. I heard (either on the radio or from the newspaper) about a concert at a church that I was vaguely aware of but knew no one that attended there. I was so desperate, that at the last moment, I gathered up my children and set out for the church. I cannot remember the name or where it was located but I know I had to drive some distance in unfamiliar territory. As the music began, I felt that I made a wrong choice. People there were happy, worshipping and praising God and I felt miserable and unworthy. Not long after the concert began, someone in the congregation began to speak in an unknown tongue and everything became silent. Then the interpretation came: "My child, I have known you since before you were conceived and I have desired your praises. I have loved you since your mother's womb and I have desired your praises. Now, I *will* walk with you through death and afterwards, I will strengthen you. *Behold, I desire your praises.*" The silence was deafening. I expected someone to shout out, fall on their knees, or perhaps, run to the altar, but nothing happened. To my eternal shame I just sat there quietly, knowing that the message was for me. After a few moments, the pastor stepped up to the pulpit and with a question in his voice proclaimed, "God has broken into this service to give a message to one of his saints," and then he began to pray. There was a time of awe inspired worship before the scheduled concert continued. As long as I live I will never ever forget that message and will never cease to wonder why I have had such a difficult time staying true to my purpose on this earth. "God, please forgive me for my stupidity."

There Are Roses in the Garden

"There are beautiful roses in my garden and some have to be crushed to appreciate their full fragrance." These words were spoken to me by my pastor as he laid hands on me. It had been about two weeks since I lost my son, Timothy. For those two weeks I had attended a service *somewhere* every single day. This particular service was powerful and anointed. When the service was seemingly over and the altar call had begun, the pastor asked for everyone to line up as he felt that the Lord wanted him to minister to each person individually, no small task since there were about four hundred or more in attendance. The line was long and by the time I got to him, an hour or more had passed. Someone had gotten him a chair and he was obviously physically tired but the Holy Spirit in him was still going strong. As I got closer and was able to hear the powerful prophecies coming forth, I became more and more expectant. The message I received was detailed and I wish I could remember it all. The one thing that stuck in my mind though was the crushing of the rose. I was happy to be a rose in God's garden but I was not happy about being crushed. Even though I didn't understand why this was happening to me, I still felt blessed that God would take the time to minister to me. It felt as if the whole service was for me as I'm sure it felt for everyone else. Later, this wonderful man of God collapsed, but only after he had prayed for every single person. It was related to me that as some of the men of the church were picking him up and planning to whisk him away to the hospital, that he admonished them and refused to go. Most of us have so little faith that even after a great move like that, we want to limit our God. He has to be amused, if not disappointed, in our weakness.

I *Still* Love You

It had been a few weeks since Timothy's home going. I was having a particularly rough time and found myself praying all day. In addition to the grief, which can only be understood by someone in the same situation, I was experiencing tremendous guilt over not being able to cope. I heard from well-meaning friends about others who had dealt with similar grief but were able to portray Godly strength. There was the couple, a great man and woman of God, who were at the church praying within hours of their loss. They visited my husband and me when we were in the hospital, in our separate rooms, I, admitted for shock and he because he had passed out from grief. I could not measure up and it was causing so much stress that I was unable to function. I attempted to do the mundane things to keep the household running but I couldn't stop crying. The prayers were tortuous and pleading. I tried to praise but just kept saying the same prayer over and over. I tried to intercede for my family but all I could say was "I'm sorry, please forgive me and give me peace, and please don't stop loving me." The same words over and over from morning to night. That evening when the family was home, I ceased to pray aloud but it was ever in my mind. During dinner, my twelve-year-old asked if I would drive her to the youth service and of course I agreed. It was a rather long drive to our church, so I joined the other parents who were in the same situation at the back of the sanctuary. There we watched and enjoyed the service though not actively participating. All the while, my prayer was still going, like a recorder in my mind, over and over. At the end of the service, the youth were asked to come to the altar to pray. Then the youth pastor did something a little out of the ordinary and asked the parents to join their children at the front of the church. There was intense praise and worship all around me and for all practical purposes it appeared I was a part of it, but inside my head was the same prayer. "God, please forgive me, give me peace, and please don't stop loving me." Then the pastor walked to the pulpit and said, "There is someone here who has been praying for an answer today and God wants to touch you." That statement pricked my heart and I thought, "I should respond," but I didn't. I reasoned with myself that someone had counseled with the pastor that day, thus the unusual train of events. After some time of exhortation for the person to reveal themselves, the pastor spoke out with such anointing and surety that the sanctuary became silent. "God is going to reveal the person to me." With that statement he looked straight toward me. I was about three or four people back from the altar with others all around me. He made a path through the worshipers and when he reached me, he said, "You're the one." With that, he placed his hand on my head and began to prophesy. What were his words? "I am the Lord, your God, I will give you peace and I *still* love you." Exactly this, no more and no less; what a great and marvelous Savior we serve.

Genesis 38

Crying out to God, I was desperate and pleading, "Please, God, show me something, anything." And with that I picked up the bible, opened it and my eyes fell on the thirty-eighth chapter of Genesis, although at the time I didn't catch the chapter and didn't even know what book I was in. I was pregnant again, way too soon, and my emotions and hormones were out of whack. To keep going and be able to function for my family, I had to depend on answered prayer for strength in both my physical body and mental state.

My mornings were filled with five children that needed to be fed, dressed and taken to school. My youngest had just begun first grade so I had full days to mourn. God had been with me in such powerful ways during that time and I experienced many much needed glorious encounters. On that particular day, I was in a very low mood as I began to read about Judah, his marriage and the birth of his three sons. As the story unfolds, Judah chooses a wife, Tamar, for his firstborn son. When his son died at the hands of God, he gave his second son to Tamar in order to raise up seed for his brother. Onan also died by the hand of God. I kept reading but I was very troubled. Why would God give me this word in my time of need? My brain was wandering, maybe God was telling me he wanted more praise since Judah is known for praise. Then as I continued reading, I found that through a series of circumstances that Judah had relations with his daughter-in-law, Tamar. I could find no good in this sinful and dark passage of scripture. I faithfully read to the end and Tamar conceived twins, Pharez and Zerah. I grabbed on to this final revelation and in my delusion and pain I told myself that I would have twins which gave me some solace at that time.

Mark and Mary Became Mark Then He Was Stillborn

After believing that I had been assured by God that I would bring twins into this world, I named them Mark and Mary. It was in the early seventies and mothers didn't know in advance the gender of her baby before birth. I just assumed that it would be a boy and a girl. I so wanted both of them and wanted to believe that I would be blessed with two babies after losing my precious Timothy. The doctor never said that I was carrying more than one baby in my womb but I held onto what I believed was a promise from God.

About five months into the pregnancy, I began to have trouble. I knew something was wrong as I lie there crying on the examination table and my obstetrician looked at me and tried to calm me down by telling me he could hear the placenta even though he couldn't pick up the heart beat and I needed to give it some time. Later that day, a friend made an appointment for me to see her specialist. He made me feel better right away by letting me listen to the birth sounds and explaining how he would get oxygen to my womb because the baby was small. He said a lot of things to assure me but the next morning he called, and in a very sorrowful voice, explained that my baby was dead. I was in shock but carried on the next few weeks believing that a miracle could still happen but it didn't. Labor pains for a stillborn child are excruciating and so different from a live birth. After delivery, I pressured the doctor into telling me the baby's sex. When I learned that it was a boy, Mark, it became very real even though they never let me see him. I went into a deep dark period that I almost didn't conquer and would not have survived without a loving God. For months I fought depression and terrible thoughts of suicide but all the while holding on to the only thing that kept me going and wondering how any human being can make it through tough times without faith in Almighty God.

Have Thine Own Way, Lord, or Do You

When I was pregnant with Timothy I began to feel closer and closer to my Lord. God had already showed me his miraculous power by healing me of my horrible indigestion and reflux. The song "Have Thine Own Way, Lord" was constantly on my mind. I sang in the bath, walking around cleaning the house, cooking and serving my children, and every time I got in the car. No adults were ever present. I only sing in front of young children. During that time, my husband was working two jobs so I had plenty of singing time. I thought it rather odd that it was the only song I sang for a period of time. It had been a long time since I had heard the tune, and it had not been sung at the church we were now attending, so it was natural for the girls to ask me, "Why are you always singing that song, we don't know it." I was in the car backing out of the driveway when that question was proposed. I was singing it and hadn't even realized until the question popped out of their mouths. It made me stop and think. I was so happy because evidently God was letting me know that I was finally following after him, and allowing him to mold me and make me after his will. I felt ecstatic and continued to spontaneously sing the same words long after my baby boy came into my life. I felt closer to the Lord than ever, having received the gift of speaking in tongues, a glorious experience, not long before Timothy was born. Then after his death, I no longer sang... *at all*. During this devastating time I attended a church service every evening drawing strength to make it through the night. I did receive blessings abundantly. Then, gradually, things were getting back to a somewhat normal life. There were kids to take to school, homework, meals, and everything that comes with family including a new pregnancy. When Mark was stillborn, the devastation turned into a deep depression, one that I could not shake. I would attend church and weep the whole service. There were no glorious messages and marvelous words that made me feel better this time. One Sunday morning, we were having a service not unlike other Sunday morning services, except that a visiting minister was in the audience and he was invited to sit on the platform with the other pastors. My heart was crying out to God and asking for relief from my misery when the visiting minister suddenly stood up and started giving a word to the church body. I had heard tongues and interpretation while attending services but never just a word of wisdom or prophesy. He was so forceful and dynamic, there was no doubt that God was speaking through him. As he prophesied, I was silently praying that I would get a word to help ease my pain and I *knew* instantly that I would hear from God. What followed was not what I expected. Suddenly, he boomed out in a loud firm voice, "My child, I speak to you personally." I listened expectantly. The next words were, "Thou *has not* been clay in my hands but if you seek me, I will reveal myself unto you." I was shocked. How could that be? Hadn't I always been good, yet I knew God was speaking to me. The congregation broke out in that hymn that had become so much a part of my life, "Have Thine Own Way" so I went to the altar and attempted to turn everything over to him. I thought he wanted me to give up and say, "Take all my kids and take everything I have." I did say that. I said everything I could think of to say as I cried and asked him what he wanted of me. Hadn't I given up enough? I didn't understand how this could happen. After I was home, I began to think of the other part of the message, "If you seek me, I will reveal myself to you." I had new hope. I would just seek him. I would like to say I did just that but the week went by with life's happenings and I was back at church repenting because I had done nothing that I thought I should have. During the service, I was in torment. I felt like my body was being ripped apart. I made a new commitment to really seek him with all my heart but the next week was the same as was the week after that. For several weeks, I continued in the same pattern until I realized that when I was at home and not dwelling on the spiritual, I seemed to feel okay but as soon as I started on my way to church and after I arrived there, I was in torment. My husband stopped attending services as soon as we lost our son, I had been attending with my children for several months without him, so I just quit going. Me, who had never even had an *ounce* of sympathy for a backslider, just quit going after twenty-eight years of nonstop attendance. I don't know if my Heavenly Father thought I was crazy then, but I would *like* to think that he felt an eternal love and sympathy for me

Romans 8:38–39 say, *"For I am persuaded, that neither death, nor life, nor angels, nor principalities, nor powers, nor things present, nor things to come, nor height, nor depth, nor any other creature, shall be able to separate us from the love of God, which is in Christ Jesus our Lord."*

Miracles

God Is Good
And Who Said You Have Ulcers
She Looks Just Like Timothy

God Is Good and "Who Said You Have Ulcers?"

Just as I was leaving my office at the chamber of commerce one evening, the phone began ringing and I heard a friend's voice on the other end saying "God is good." My friend was just being discharged from the hospital with these words from the doctor, "Your heart is perfect, your liver is perfect and your cholesterol is great," he said, "just think if I hadn't gone to the hospital with this freak thing, I wouldn't have known that God had healed me." He reminded me of the summer before when they said that both his heart and liver were bad. He and a pastor friend of ours, prayed for his complete healing and deliverance. He was praising God, while still in his voice was that familiar element of surprise and excitement that said, I asked for it, I prayed for and it really happened. This took me back to a similar incidence in my own life. It was in early summer almost a year after I lost Timothy and a couple of months since the birth of my stillborn son, Mark. Dr. Painter with the Ledbetter Clinic was looking at me incredulously as he asked the question "Who said you have ulcers?" I was lying in a hospital bed, a little groggy from all the medicine given to me for various tests. I had been seriously depressed and the gynecologist had prescribed antidepressants. With my mental state all out of whack, my body reacted with some physical symptoms that landed me in the hospital. An upper and lower GI was one of the many tests that were performed. It was after these procedures that the doctor was sitting on the side of my bed giving me a good report on my intestines. I asked him how my ulcer scars looked when he asked *the* question. I was a little shocked. I had never been questioned before and certainly not with such an attitude of disbelief. He was asking me "what hospital," "doctor's name," "how long," as if he just couldn't comprehend what I was telling him. When I answered all of his questions, he just patted my leg through the blanket, smiled sweetly and said, "Your stomach is as pink as a new born babe's." He left the room and just then the phone rang. I heard my good friend's voice call my name and I said to her, "I think God has healed my ulcers." She called my name a few times and then realized that I had passed out in sleep. I woke up later with the phone by my ear and that is when the realization of God's power overwhelmed me. He had made a clean sweep. When he healed me of my digestive problems during my pregnancy, he gave me a new stomach. That's why there were no old scars and that is why Dr. Painter said my stomach looked like a new born babe's. It *was* new. And, as I pondered on it, I recalled that I was no longer in the habit of carting Pepto-Bismol around and what about the Mexican food I was eating for the first time in my life and enjoying it. And funny how, for someone that had lived with stomach aches all of those years, I had not had any for some time. I could not understand why God healed me and took away something that had plagued me all of my life, only then to take my two precious babies. I still don't understand.

She Looks Just Like Timothy

I lifted up and rested on the elbow of one arm as I mumbled "she looks just like Timothy" and then, just as quickly, I laid my head back down in a drug induced sleep. I was being wheeled out of labor and delivery toward my room when they stopped the bed at the window of the nursery. With me was my sweet mom, a wonderful Christian friend and of course, my husband, daddy of the beautiful little girl that had just been held up for me to see. It was all so obvious, they were going on and on about the beautiful baby girl I had just given birth to. I knew they were worried about my mental state. I had been worried too. For the last two or three months, I had been praying over and over, "Please, God, if I have a daughter, please, please don't let me develop postpartum depression." I had heard so much about it and the effect it had, not only on the new mother but on the development of the baby as well. I had gone into this pregnancy with mixed up hormones and a troubled mind, so for the first five months the only thoughts I had were for the safety of the baby I was carrying. I was so distraught with worry and fear that something would go wrong that I declined a baby shower. Then when it looked as if everything was going well and I would make it to term, this new fear started gnawing at me. I so wanted another boy.

When I was fully awake and the nurse brought my precious baby girl to me (the joy and light of my life), I looked down at the beautiful little bundle in my arms and had to chuckle aloud when I thought of the reactions that surely had gone on earlier after my comment at the nursery window. My visitors were gone now and although I hadn't meant to alarm them, I knew they were probably still anxious over my comment. My prayers were answered and I couldn't even remember the concern or fear that I felt earlier. Could it be that God gets lots of chuckles because of all our worry when he has everything under control.

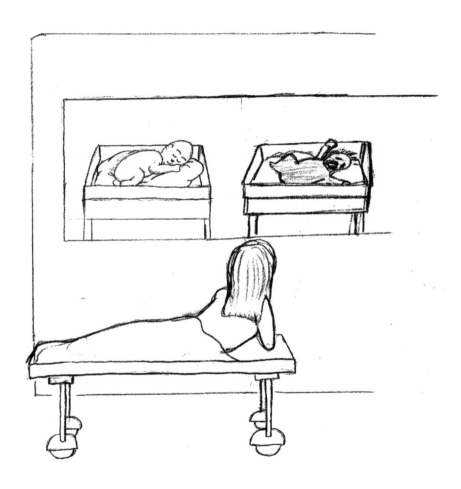

Coming Back

Backsliders? Pleeeeease...

I could never understand anyone that would leave their provider, Jehovah Jireh, their supplier, El Shaddai, their healer, Jehovah Rophe, their Father, Jehovah Lord God, and their very best friend and Savior, Jesus Christ. It didn't make sense and seemed stupid to me. I've loved God since I can remember and always wanted to serve him. I knew that I was supposed to feel overjoyed when someone that had left the presence of God came back into the fold, but I had no real sympathy. I felt they should never have left.

Then, life happened to me and I fell apart, but my Father, my best friend, held me up. He was there in every direction that I took and every dark hole that I climbed in. I had direct contact to heaven for a time with divine messages and impartations. Then, I gradually pulled away. I was given the gift of a wonderful and precious daughter. There were no complications; she was perfect. There was absolutely no reason for me to leave the presence of the Almighty, yet I had and didn't even realize it. When my baby girl was about two years of age, I was driving to our place of business one day, listening to country western music, something I had never been interested in. Gospel music was the only thing that had ever appealed to me, the only thing that I listened to, or sang when I was alone or with children, small enough that they wouldn't care or know if I were off key. It was as if I woke up suddenly, out of a fog. The Spirit pricked at my heart. I couldn't remember when it happened. It was all so gradual that I didn't know when the complete change had occurred.

I began to weep as I was driving when I realized that it had been a year or more since I had spoken to my friend, Elohim, my creator. In the past, I always communicated with him even if just a few words. It had been at least two years since I had sat in a church service. I could not conceive how that happened to me. I turned off the radio and tried to sing old familiar songs until I reached the Exxon service station that we owned. I put it in the back of my mind until that evening when I was alone in my bedroom and I asked God to let me know if it was not too late. I was concerned that I had grieved the Holy Spirit and didn't know how to come back. At the very moment that I finished my question, my eight-year-old son called out to me from his bedroom at the other end of the house. When I walked in, he was on his knees beside the bed and he asked me to pray with him. I knew then that my Father was taking me back. The whole family was drawn to him during the next few days and we all went to church the next Sunday. It was so glorious to be back. What an humbling experience. It taught me that only by the grace of God, can we be called the sons and daughters of the Almighty and not by our works of righteousness.

Take Him off the Cross, She Cried

I was in the kitchen and my four-year-old daughter walked in, sobbing hysterically. "Mama, Jesus was on the cross and I tried to hide him in the closet but you got him back out," her face contorted in pain as she paused and then continued, "I kept saying take him off the cross but you wouldn't." I knew God had used my small child to reach me through her dream.

For some time, I had been unable to forgive myself for not following through on what I felt I was called to do. I wasn't exactly sure what "it" was but I just "knew" that I had failed in God's original plan for my life. In church, I would tell God that I was sorry for my failures, then I would be sorry for "being sorry." I became tortured and obsessed with not being able to forgive myself and then knowing that I was going against what I had been taught, and believed with all of my heart. The finished work of the cross was permanent and I could rely on God's forgiveness when I asked.

I was like someone with a mental illness that originated in my spirit causing my mind to replay the same requests over and over.

The day before, in the Sunday morning service, the gift of tongues and interpretation had come forth with an admonition to those that "crucify the Son of God afresh" found in Hebrews 6:6. When I heard it I became even more convicted. I did not want to displease my Savior whom I loved. That afternoon, I flipped through the scriptures looking for the passage that held those words. That night in the evening service, I was going through my tortuous ritual again, sorry and then sorry for being sorry. I frantically looked again and found the scripture. Even though I was obsessively repenting over and over, I was also asking God to break this pitiful and satanic hold on me.

It is so miraculous how God works. As I contemplated on the meaning of my baby's dream and the great lengths God will use to reach his children, I was completely delivered. That was it. The ordeal was over.

"Thank You for Turning That Off"

My oldest son's words were tortured as he thanked me for turning his radio off. I had assumed he was asleep as it was not time to start his day when I walked into his room with an agitated urgency and flicked off the switch. My state of mind resulted from his continuous habit of leaving his radio on all night. I usually turned it off in the middle of the night but this time I did not, which in itself was unusual on my part as I passed by his room several times that night with trips to the bathroom and kitchen for water for a sleepless daughter. When I walked in, the other part of my urgency was from the music that was playing. The only way that I can describe what I heard was that it had a mystical, very demonic or evil sound to it. As I felt panicked to get it shut off, I was thinking to myself that it must be very popular because it was the same song that I had heard every time I passed by. As my son pulled his head out from under the covers and thanked me, he said, "That song has been playing all night long." Of course, I questioned him on why he just didn't get up and turn it off and I wanted to know if that was a popular piece of music (I don't think it had any words). He said he had never heard it before. I could tell that he was truly upset and though we didn't talk about it anymore, I noticed that he started listening to more upbeat and moral music. He was a teenager at the time and we had conversations more than once about his choice of music. I never had to speak to him again about the music he listened to. God can take care of anything. Even if Satan meant if for harm, God turned it into good. Thank you, Lord.

The Dog and the Vision

I was lying down in the back of our van trying to sleep. It was summertime *hot* in Texas. My younger son and my baby, my daughter (who were asleep), had traveled with me to our church's camp meeting. To save money, we were sleeping in the van at the campground. As I was lying there thinking about the service we had just attended, there appeared before my eyes, almost to the ceiling of the vehicle, a series of what appeared to be buildings. It reminded me of a quick rendering of a city with rectangular and square shapes, some tall and some shorter. I began to hear a ticking sound that matched the hyphen marks that I saw going in and out of the buildings. In my mind, I was saying, what does this mean, God? Suddenly the little city was gone and in its' place appeared the image of a ceramic dog that we had purchased in Mexico. On top of the dog's head was a tiny casket and as it opened. I began to cry out to God, "Please don't make me look." Then it was gone and I was lying there staring at the ceiling. I slept fitfully after that, if at all, and as soon as the sun came up, I made my way to the pay phone. I felt such fear that I called my husband, who was to join me that day along with my oldest son. I related what had happened and begged him to be especially careful driving in. He didn't say much but I could tell that he felt whatever I felt. They arrived safely and I tried to put the fear out of my mind. I felt the ticking was a clock and that God was telling me that we were running out of time to help those that were lost and needed him. I presumed that, maybe, the coffin was something to let me know how serious this was.

About two weeks after we were home from camp meeting and I was going about my regular routine, I was interrupted by my little granddaughter running up to me and crying hysterically about my youngest child. I couldn't understand what she was saying but I heard "blood" and I knew that my baby was hurt. I immediately ran to her and what I found was a bloody face and a scared, crying little girl. We grabbed her up and headed to the hospital, her daddy driving and me holding her with pressure on her chin to keep the bleeding to a minimum. By that time, I knew that she was jumping on my bed and fell on the dog that was in my vision. My husband and I drove to the hospital in silence but my thoughts were crying out to God. I was saying, "Please don't let anything happen to her." And all the while I was thinking, surely you can't die from a cut. My thoughts were wild as I thought of the little coffin. I told myself it would be impossible and then I thought of all the serious infections that can come from a wound. Mentally, I was a mess. She got three stitches and all seemed well as we were driving home, though I was still questioning the meaning of it all. Suddenly my husband blurted out, "I almost got rid of that dog when we came home." And then I knew that I wasn't the only one that was lost in thought and fear.

When we arrived at the house, my two sons were waiting in the yard with worried looks on their little faces, that told me that they, too, had the feeling that something was not "quite right." The oldest said, quite matter of factly, that he had taken a sledge hammer and beat the dog into smithereens. Did the ceramic dog have some spirits attached to it from a different, sometimes Godless, culture or was this a way to draw attention to our earthly mission. We should witness in the highways and hedges *and* buildings of the city. Do I feel like that I heeded that warning? No, I never feel that I have been used as I should be but I will never forget that ticking of the clock and it is always on my mind when I donate to missionaries and to evangelists that win more souls than I could ever talk to in a lifetime. Whatever God thinks of me, I just hope he is a little pleased with my efforts because I love him and adore him beyond what I can express with my words.

The Lost Hearing Aid

Please God, I sobbed, as I stumbled down the dirt road. Please, please let me find that hearing aid. My youngest son was born with a hearing loss. He made it into junior high school by sheer grit. He missed a lot but he concentrated and was an excellent lip reader. Technology had improved from the box in his pocket with a wire leading up to his ear that we had tried in his first year of school so when he was fourteen he was fitted with a hearing aid. Even though the doctor advised that he have one in each ear for optimum benefit, his daddy agreed to buy him only one. We were getting closer to convincing my husband that we should invest in the second aid when my son called me from school to tell me that he couldn't find his hearing aid. He had missed it that morning but thought he left it in the locker when he took it out of his ear to play baseball. He couldn't hear me well enough on the phone to answer my questions but told me the events of the evening before. His older brother was driving and they gave a ride to a friend that lived down the road about a mile from us. He thought that it was possible that the aid was wrapped up in the jacket that he had removed and was accidentally dropped in Benji's driveway because that was the only place they had stopped on the way home. I knew that if we didn't find the hearing aid, that not only would there be no second aid purchased, but the first one would not be replaced. I stumbled out of the house, crying out to God, I tried to look as I walked but by the time that I reached the dirt road, red when the sun shined just right, but barely pink that morning, my eyes were so full of tears that I could barely make my way. I felt helpless but headed to the neighbor's driveway while trying to look on the road. With every petition to God to find the aid, I felt it was hopeless. I was about a third of the way to their home when I struggled to open my eyes to see where I was. I had my hands on my face trying to wipe the tears. I looked down and there it was, in the tire ruts, in the fleshy colored sand, the exact color of the hearing aid. I picked it up and walked back praising God with my hands lifted in the air. There is no other explanation than God placed that aid in the road right in front of me. The tire ruts were deep and everyone drove in them. It was easier than staying out of them on the narrow road. Several cars had traveled the road that morning heading out to the main highway. I will always wonder if the hearing aid got dropped out of the locker somewhere in school or fell out in Benji's driveway but I know without a doubt that wherever it was, my wonderful Lord put it there at that moment for me to find.

This Young Lady Has a Broken Neck

I was sitting there in disbelief. The doctor had stopped talking to me after he dropped the fourth X-ray into one of the frames lined across his wall. He seemed alarmed as he called for his nurse to come in. It seemed as if everything went into slow motion as I heard him say, "Patrick, get her husband in here, this young lady has a broken neck." How, I thought, could this be real? I was afraid to move yet I had been moving. I walked into the doctor's office. I climbed on the X-ray table. My mind was racing. "When you have a broken neck, aren't you paralyzed."

I went to Dr. Hassman for a second opinion after I had been in our small town hospital for two weeks. I fell off our sunroof while attempting to move a mattress out of the top floor bedroom, which opened onto the roof, down to the truck at the bottom of the stairs. My son went first and stopped on the landing as I reached for the first step. The mattress was blocking my vision and I lifted it so I could see and then lowered it. Somehow I missed the step. I still don't remember the fall down and when I woke up in the hospital later, I did not have any memory of the event. The lapse of memory lasted for several days and I was diagnosed with a broken back in two places and six broken ribs.

I had been out of the hospital for a couple of weeks when it was time for my husband to go for a six months check up for a back

69

surgery. Dr. Hassman was a specialist in another city about an hours' drive away. I was still in a lot of pain especially across the top part of my back right below my neck. I felt that the hospital team only did the minimum, focusing on wherever I said it hurt so when I walked into Dr. Hassman's office, I just simply said, "I fell off of our roof and I want to be checked." They were very thorough and X-rayed me from head to toe. It was these X-rays the doctor was looking at while asking me what the hospital told me and calmly agreeing with some of the diagnosis until he stopped and called his nurse in. I tried to listen and concentrate as he explained everything to my husband. He pointed to the X-ray that clearly showed a very broken bone with a jagged edge at the point where it was broken and tilted out of place. It had already begun to heal and had somehow missed the nerves that were entwined in and around. It was explained that the first option would have been to put needles in my head and use a procedure that would have straightened the bone as it was healing but since that was not an option now, he wanted to make sure it was stable and then fuse a bone from another place in my body. I was sent home with a neck brace, Percodan (strong pain medicine), and orders for no physical activity and to keep my neck still for a week. I stayed in the bed day and night. I had a fear of being sick and causing damage from even the slightest movement so I lived on Coca-Cola. At my check up, I was uplifted when I was told that I had a strong grip. My doctor was smiling when he told me everything was stable. I chose to wait on surgery and wore the neck brace for several months while continuing to have a lot of pain. My neck felt so weak that I couldn't sit in a chair without a high back to rest my head on. During my six month check-up, I was encouraged to have the surgery due to a much better chance for success at my age rather than waiting until I was older. I chose to wait a little longer. At my one year revisit, another X-ray revealed a crooked bone with a lot of arthritis all around it. I asked, "If I make it five years, then do you think it is a good chance that I will make it without having surgery." He laughed and these were his words, "Before five years have expired, you will be *begging* me for surgery," with a strong emphasis on the word begging. For some time, I had been holding my neck with first one hand and then the other, saying, "God please heal my neck, I am afraid of surgery." I did it around the house when I was alone and while driving around in my car. Gradually everything got back to "normal." My neck seemed stronger and stronger. I quit holding it all of the time and even though I was grateful that it wasn't bothering me, it was easy to forget about what happened. I was charging around as always, getting things done, running businesses taking care of children and now grandchildren when my back went out and I made an appointment with a chiropractic doctor. He was a Christian and wanted to pray for me before he started his treatment. I was eager for that and we began to talk. I started to tell him about my neck and how God had kept me from pain. I noticed that he looked a little surprised. As a matter of routine, he had taken X-rays. He commented that he hadn't noticed anything out of the ordinary when he glanced over them before he came in for our consultation. I asked to see them and to my astonishment the neck bone looked to be completely straight. I didn't see any of the signs that Dr. Hassman had showed me of the arthritis. I was bewildered and he seemed to be too, as he said, "There is nothing that even indicates that there has been any trauma." I would like to be able to explain why I prayed for something so fervently and then be so surprised when it happens. I think God has to be a little amused at his creation when they are like me.

His Presence

5:30 AM… Reaaally
Daryl's Angels
It looked and Felt like the "Good Life"
God, This Is Ridiculous
Ruth
Leave Her Alone
Just Ask God, Mom, He Will Help You
She Stood There Quietly Trying to Overcome Her Fear
The Good Will Store
Leave Her Alone, Roger, She's in Heaven Right Now

5:30 AM... Reeeally?

I tried to reason with God as I spoke in my spirit. Six in the morning would be plenty early and 6:30 a.m. would be even better. That timing would go so much better with my morning duties. If I arose at 5:30 and prayed for thirty minutes then I would have thirty to forty-five minutes of void time. Not enough time to go back to bed and too early to wake up anyone for school, so yes, I agreed with myself that 6:30 would be fine and I set my clock for what I thought was the agreed upon time but the next morning when my eyes popped open and I was instantly wide awake, I looked at the clock and it was 5:30. So, I thought, I love the Holy Spirit's sense of humor. My prayer time was great and I didn't have any time to waste. After several days of setting my alarm for 6:30 and then becoming fully awake at 5:30, I conceded that the Lord God of the universe wanted me to obey. Even though we can't sometimes understand the reasoning behind God's demands, obedience is a priority with him.

This prayer time went on for several years with some mornings where all I could do was roll out and get on my knees by the bed and praise God while half asleep but some mornings were glorious. Then one day, I felt God releasing me from this morning ritual. There was no prewarning in my Spirit. It just happened. Total release in one instant. I can't explain the feeling of relief that I had after getting up every morning for so long, even on the weekend. I was excited and totally at peace. I could sleep late and that sounded so heavenly to me.

After about a week of "freedom," I realized how much I actually missed that prayer time. I was hit or miss for a few years but because of the assurance I had and the total peace in my heart, the times that I spent with my Lord were indescribable. In less than five years, God began dealing with me again about prayer and this time it included fasting and yes, the time was still 5:30.

"And Samuel said, Hath the LORD *as great* delight in burnt offerings and sacrifices, as in obeying the voice of the LORD? Behold, to obey *is* better than sacrifice, *and* to hearken than the fat of rams." (1 Sam. 15:22)

Daryl's Angels

My youngest son watched me intently as I studied the tract he handed me and as he turned to leave my home office, he asked, "what are you thinking?" And I answered, "Probably the same thing you are thinking." And with that, he looked directly at me and said with a question in his voice, "Angels?"

My aunt (my mother's sister) had been recently diagnosed with leukemia. My two brothers and I decided to organize a prayer meeting especially for her. A day was designated and it was announced in church that anyone who wanted to help us pray were welcome to come. From the first week, we had a good attendance, and more needs were brought for prayer than just my aunt's. This prayer meeting became a scheduled service and continued for so long that there came a time when no one but us knew how, why or when the prayer time was originally started. The meetings were so successful that we had visitors attending and many special needs were met, but my most memorable experience occurred in the very beginning. On the second week of prayer, I came in about 7:30 and knelt down with others around me and began to pray for my aunt. About five minutes into my prayer, the familiar warmth of the Holy Spirit came upon me. I suddenly blurted out, aloud, "God, be with Daryl right now and bless him." That was all I said and it was over. In that short minute, I had time to think "how could God bless him right now, he is working at the Video Store," not very conducive to interacting with the Spirit of God. Nevertheless, I made a few more requests of God to touch my son. Then I resumed my prayer for my aunt and the prayer meeting ended that night, rather uneventfully for me. Early the next morning the phone rang and on the other end was the very emotional voice of my son asking, "Were you praying for me last night?" He had no idea that I was at a prayer meeting; unfortunately our busy schedules left little time for sharing. My answer was yes, although, had it not been for the Spirit of God, the answer would have been no. He then asked, "What time, do you remember?" And of course I did because it was at the beginning so I responded, "About 7:35." There was silence on the other end of the phone and when he did speak, it was with great difficulty and with much emotion as he began to recount his experiences from the night before. A lady came into our video store that he had never seen before nor has seen to this day. She started witnessing to him about the Lord and how he needed to get ready and stay ready to meet him. After a while, she suddenly blurted out, "Where is your mother?" And as he nodded and said he didn't know, she exclaimed in a bold voice, "She is at church and right now, she is praying for you." He said he thought that was a little strange because he knew there was no scheduled worship service on Tuesday nights but she was so emphatic that he glanced at the clock on the wall and it was exactly 7:35. He recounted that she stayed with him until he closed at 9:00 p.m. She followed him and talked all the time, while he returned movies to their shelves and went through his regular nightly closing duties. She walked out the door with him as he locked up. Strange, he thought, as he left the store, she never rented a movie or even looked for one. On the way home, and still a little unsettled by the unusual visit, he stopped at a convenience store. He was stopped in an aisle and looking for his purchase when he became aware of a black gentleman stopped in front of him. The man had a brochure in his hand and was offering it to him as he said something like "I am supposed to give you this" or possibly "I need to give you this." Daryl took it and read, "Are you ready to meet

God." He immediately looked up and there was no one in sight. He franticly searched, going quickly down each aisle in the small store, but the stranger was nowhere to be found. With that startling bit of information, my son then hung up the phone, and left me to ponder these events. Soon, he was at my home with the tract that was given him the night before. The little brochure was not unlike many church tracts I have seen before with a message and scriptures to back it up. Most religious organizations have them in abundance. But this one did not have the familiar stamp of a church on the back. I searched it completely. There was no contact name of a person or organization, no one to call except God himself. After Daryl opened the store and got everything settled, he called and informed me that a young family friend had called when he first arrived and invited him to a service at his church that night. I asked him if he was going and he responded with "How can I. I have to close tonight." I decided to go. It was a very enjoyable and informative service. What was the title of the message preached by the evangelist that night? *Angels* and how they are in our midst and serving and ministering to us, seen and unseen.

Ps. 91:11 states, "For he shall give his angels charge over thee, to keep thee in all of thy ways."

Luke 4:10 states, "For it is written, He shall give his angels charge over thee, to keep thee."

It Looked and Felt Like the "Good Life"

In the late eighties, we were doing well financially, and living in a two-story home in what was considered to be a good neighborhood. Though active in church and consumed with family and living a "good life," I carried a cloud over me of feeling that I had failed to live up to my potential in God.

One night I went to sleep praying and then woke up feeling the Spirit of God so strong that I could not stay in bed. I went downstairs to the living room where the Holy Spirit was so powerful that I lay prostrate on the floor. This was not the "norm" so I knew that this would be a special time in the Lord. When that "feeling" came, to open the Bible for a word, I immediately obeyed. The pages fell open to Jeremiah in the first chapter and I began to read. I got to the fifth verse, "Before I formed thee in the belly, I knew thee; and before thou camest forth out of the womb, I sanctified thee, and I ordained thee a prophet unto the nations." Immediately my mind went back eighteen years to these words, "My child, I have known you since before you were conceived and I have desired your praises. I have loved you since your mother's womb and I have desired your praises." This was the word that I received in the little church that I attended after I lost Timothy. The rest of the prophecy was that he would walk with me through death. I couldn't control my emotions as I went back to that period in my life.

I then thought of the passage about Juda and his daughter-in-law, Tamar. From time to time that chapter had come to mind but was of no consequence to me since I didn't have twins and that was the only thing I gleaned from my reading on that long ago day. I determined that I would find that passage of scripture and dwell on it until God revealed the meaning. My Bible didn't have a concordance and I prayed and searched that night to no avail. The next morning I was in the kitchen doing dishes. I looked over to the book shelf and I knew that I was going to find that passage. I picked up the Bible and it fell open to Genesis 38. I rejoiced as I praised God for his wonderful sense of humor. He didn't let me find it. He wants to be in charge. I was overcome with desire to find out what my God wanted to tell me. I determined that I wouldn't rest until I found the meaning to that scripture.

I prayed and I asked him to reveal himself to me but then I let the worries and duties of this life take precedence once again.

God, This Is Ridiculous

"God, this is ridiculous, I *have* to be *crazy* to attempt a fast and prayer time at the end of the month when I am so busy and on deadlines. I will never again fast at this time," I whined. These words were spoken by me during a personal fast that occurred in the late eighties. In the last few days I have been reading a book about fasting and even though I haven't been on a spiritual fast in several years the memory of God intervening in my life is vivid and real. The fast began when the desire to find the meaning of the messages that I received from the Lord in earlier years had come to the surface again. "This time," I told the Lord, "I will fast and pray until I find the meaning and unravel the mystery of these ongoing messages." I fasted all day Monday, but unfortunately it was payroll time for our businesses and I could not find the time to pray except for a couple of quickies.

On Tuesday morning, still working from my home office, I was miserable and irritable as I was trying to concentrate on a form for payroll taxes. I had a terrific head ache by noon. I had the same Christian radio station on that I always kept playing but the sound of the ministers that I usually loved only made my headache worse. I got out of my chair to go and put a music tape in and I talked and whined to God all the way to the radio tape player. I grabbed a tape and stuck it in. As I settled back at my desk, I became aware of the song and the words, "A rose has to be crushed to get the full fragrance… and you are a rose in God's garden." I was half listening as I realized this beautiful song that I had never heard before was replaying words that I had heard from an earlier personal prophecy. Then it ended and before I could rise to go play it again, the second song on the tape came on and it was all about the potter's wheel and how the vessel was marred in the potter's hand and he was reshaping it. The song told a complete story and had many of the same words that had been a reoccurring theme in my life. By this time I was back at the radio and starting it over. The first song was beautiful about the rose but the second made me a little confused as I always received this message the same way. *Surely, I could not be the vessel. I had not been marred.* I listened carefully to both songs marveling that I had not heard them before. This tape had been played over and over but always the other side. How could I have overlooked them? I sat back on the sofa that was right in front of the television as I basked in yet another undeserved communication from the One that I loved so dearly. I looked at the television that was never turned on because it was used primarily by my husband and son for recording and checking the hundreds of movies that moved through this office and then to the video stores that we owned. As I stared at the blank screen, I knew I had to turn it on. The screen lit up with Efrem Zimbalist, Jr., a popular actor in the fifties and sixties. He was there, looking right at me, and he said, "Now, for our Bible reading today," then he proceeded to read Genesis 38 from beginning to end, and then closed the Bible. This message and passage of scripture had been given to me over and over and I just could not understand why. It is not the best example of Godly living. So as I sat there in awe and wonderment (I still did not know *or* could not *accept* what God was trying to tell me). I did know one thing for sure; no matter if we are a little stubborn *or* a little *crazy,* God will still honor our sacrifices. It was not a perfect fast but there was a desire made known to God at the beginning of my fast and he honored it with perfect answers. Unfortunately, the message went to an imperfect vessel.

Ruth

I couldn't shake the feeling that I needed to read the book of Ruth. I would dismiss it by telling God that I knew the story well and continued to read other passages of scripture.

During the late eighties and early nineties I was consumed with our businesses and raising my teenage daughter, my baby. The older children were married and on their own and grandchildren were being born. Even though I still had those moments of feeling like God had been trying to tell me something for years and I just couldn't quite get it, my love for him was steady and strong. One day, the desire became so pressing that I needed to read Ruth that I thought, "Okay, I'll just read it and get it over with and then I can go on to something else." It is a wonderful story and of course I enjoyed it even though I could tell it from memory. Then something happened, I got to the last chapter and verse 18 says, "Now these are the generations of Pharez." My mind was spinning. Could this be the same Pharez, the twin that was born to Judah and Tamar? This lineage produced Boaz, Obed (the son of Ruth and Boaz), Jesse, and King David. Our Lord Jesus was proclaimed to be in the lineage of King David. I cannot convey the condition of my mind and heart for the next few days. I was thoughtful, quiet, and confused, almost in a depressed state. In all those years I tried to make something mysterious about God's words to me but could Genesis 38 have simply been God's way of telling me that no matter what mistakes we make or what sins we commit that he can turn it around for good when we are a true worshiper? Judah means praise and I knew that and now I know that no matter how low Judah became in my eyes for his sin, God took that union and that line to produce the Son of God so there is hope for all of us.

Leave Her Alone!

There were five of us in a circle and we were praying for my daughter. A friend cried out, "Leave her alone." Her cry was angry as she stamped her foot on the floor. I was ashamed as these four women interceded for my loved one. They were actually angry at Satan for something that I had just accepted.

Earlier in the evening, several of us gathered in my neighborhood clubhouse to pray. I tired after about an hour and joined another lady to quietly talk. We talked about several things and I shared with her how my daughter had been bothered, and actually attacked by Satan since she was just a baby. During our conversation, I became aware of a lady who had a reputation for being a prayer warrior; she was fervently praying and occasionally calling out "Yes, Lord." Soon, the other ladies got off their knees one by one and were quietly talking, a couple of them took their leave and then there were just four of us left. The sister who was so engrossed in conversation with God was still on her knees, eyes wide open but seemingly unaware of anything going on. Then the door opened and the friend that cried out "leave her alone" walked in. At that moment the prayer warrior jumped up and started crying over and over "Thank you, Lord." She then directed us to the clock which said 8:30 and she proceeded to tell us that God had given her the verse, "And five of you shall chase an hundred," Leviticus 26:8, and told her that a miracle would happen at 8:30. She had been a little dismayed when everyone started leaving but then the fifth person walked in. She quickly gathered us into a circle and said that God was going to perform a miracle and it was going to be big and then instructed us to pray. After a short pause, the lady I was talking to originally, blurted out that my daughter, who was eighteen at the time, had been attacked by Satan her whole life. The faithful, praying saint shouted "that's it" and proceeded to lead the rest of us in prayer and it *was* powerful prayer. As undeserving as I felt at the time, my sweet daughter was delivered from torment that night. When I told her later what had happened, she received the word with no hesitation. Even though there had been attempts in the past to pray against this evil with some relief from time to time, this night was different and Satan was totally cast off from her life. God has to wonder why we accept and endure things when he has given us so much power in his name.

Just Ask God, Mom, He Will Help You

My teenage daughter, my baby, was so sincere as she tried to lift my spirits one night by encouraging me to act on my dream of writing a book. "Ask God to help you, Mom" was her reply when I impatiently said, "Baby, I haven't thought about that in a long time, I just don't think it is in me anymore." I was sitting at my desk in my home office, too drained mentally and spiritually to have any dreams anymore. I had been in a fog, a kind of depression for months. She came up to me and gently laid her hands on my shoulders as she said, "You can still do it, God will help you." I looked up at her sweet face and replied in the low monotone of the weary, "I don't even know if I want to write anymore." She looked sad and left me to my thoughts. How did I get to this point, I was the same girl that could not remember a time when God was not uppermost in my mind. I was the one who wanted to be a missionary, who wanted to write for God's Glory, who loved God with all my heart. Yet, here I was sitting here defeated. This realization only made me sadder as I cried out to God to help me. There was no instant victory felt, I was still downhearted as I retired for the evening but God was already on the job and began the process to restore me. He is so faithful.

She Stood There Quietly Trying to Overcome Her Fear

As I looked into her face, she timidly bowed her head. I knew she was the wife of a man that carried a large wooden cross on his back around the country. I had seen him locally on more than one occasion. As I looked on this plainly dressed, unassuming young woman, my conscience was pricked. Here I was, with obvious material blessings compared to this couple who certainly deserved more than I and yet my heart and mind were far from God. I attended the service of a minister friend with the intention of supporting him in his endeavor to start a new church. But my support, that evening, had only added another body to the congregation. I waited for her to say something and as she slowly raised her eyes to mine, she said, "God says, there is something that you have always wanted to do and He wants you to do it." I was dumbfounded as I had no idea that this timid little girl was going to attempt to give me a word from the Lord. I just stared as my mind was reeling off thoughts, what is it. Is it being blessed with my business? Is it a financial out pouring? After a moment, she barely raised her head and shifted uneasily as she repeated, "It is something that you have always wanted to do." I know I made her uncomfortable with my blank expression and then she asked, "Could it be writing?" I still stared blankly as my mind raced. I had thought of being a writer and made several attempts at a younger age. In the past, I had a strong desire to use my talent to honor God with Christian publications. But years of unhappiness and disappointments of life had dulled my spirit. As I just looked, she turned meekly away and went back to her seat. The service was over and every one was praying so I was able to step behind a portable blackboard and cry without anyone noticing me. I was crying, not because of the great revelation, but because I was sad that I was so spiritually unattached to my Savior that I loved. It had only been a week since my daughter tried to encourage me with this very thing and yet I was so cold, I was caught totally unaware. After I composed myself, I approached the young woman and told her she had been correct with her words. I saw how she was struggling with the decision to respond to God and I knew if I did not reassure her, she would leave doubting herself and find it difficult to follow the Spirit's prompting in the future. Her quick sweet smile proved that God had used this time to not only give me words that I needed to hear but to give her confidence and assurance so he could use her in the future. What a great, smart God that we serve.

The Good Will Store

I was in our local Good Will Store shopping for jeans and shirts in several different sizes. I had my list of sizes but was having a hard time reaching high enough on some of the shelves. The truth is, I have never been a good shopper and always get impatient looking, even for myself, and this kind of shopping was even worse. I noticed a well-dressed black man who I supposed to be the manager, and I asked him for help. He was gracious and stayed right with me until he had pulled out every single pair of jeans and shirts that I needed. While filling my list, I was chatting and explaining why I needed all these clothes. Friends, a husband and wife team, have a ministry that reaches into Mexico. They have a burden for the orphans across the border and regularly make the trip with clothes, toys and whatever they can gather. At Christmas, they coordinate local churches to give presents to the children. This was one of the times that they came up short and I was filling in the missing clothing by shopping at Good Will. As he handed me the last item on my list, I started to thank him for going the extra mile in helping me, when he looked at me and said, "You're a minister." To me, it sounded like a question and I said no. To which he replied, and said, "I didn't ask you, I said you are." He went on to explain that we are all ministers doing God's work and you didn't have to preach to be a minister. Then he said something (I don't remember what it was) but I remember what I said because I realized in that embarrassing moment that he did not work for the Good Will Store. I apologized profusely, while he smiled and told me how happy he was to help me. We talked for a little while longer and I found out his name was Clarence and that he was a music producer and was involved in various ministries. He gave me his card and even though I lost the card, I have thought a lot about Clarence and what he said to me. I still wondered why he was wandering around the store looking like he was there to help me and I assumed that one day I would find his card and contact him but to my shame, I never did. Thank you, Lord, I did need help that day.

Leave Her Alone, Roger She's in Heaven Right Now

Brother Daniel was looking intently at me as Roger walked up and asked me if I had talked to the pastor about a business that he and I were involved in.

The pastor barely turned as he laughingly said to him, "Leave her alone, Roger, she is in heaven right now." We had gone back to the church office at Roger's behest. I stuttered and couldn't even think. The truth is that I was half in this world and half out. I drove home in a daze that continued for hours. I don't remember what I was thinking and I don't remember the drive home but I do remember hearing the doorbell ring and when I answered, my son was standing there. I remember the look on his face as if he had seen a ghost as he asked me what was wrong. I fell into his arms crying, "I've been with God."

That Sunday morning had begun with a visit to a church that I had never attended and was across town in unfamiliar territory. I would never have gone just to "visit" but Roger was an associate of mine and wanted to talk to the pastor about pulling his congregation into our business. Roger knew many ministers; he had been a gospel singer for many years and regularly ministered in song on Christian TV as well as having a brother that pastored a large church. I felt honored to be associated with him, so he had no trouble in convincing me to come. He and his wife were not there when I arrived but the church was so full that I couldn't find an end seat and had to step over congregants to finally be seated in the middle of a row, a position that I was not comfortable in since I knew no one there. When Roger and his wife arrived, it was apparent that they were unaware of my presence as they made their way to the front and were seated on the second row. I soon relaxed and reveled in the spirit that was in the church. Brother Ponce was speaking on prayer but he didn't just "speak," he brought the congregation into powerful prayer. It was so moving that two hours passed quickly. I was shocked when I looked at my watch but at the same time elated because God had been dealing with me about my own prayer life. I felt the unction to start a regular fast and prayer time and had begun intercessory prayer. Just the week before, I received a letter from my own pastor asking me my opinions on the power of prayer. He stated in the letter that this was not a uniform letter and that I was one of few that was receiving it so I took it very seriously and had just mailed my answers within a couple of days of this service. What a glorious confirmation. I felt the joy of the Lord and was so glad that I had been a part of the service. Brother Ponce began to come down from his powerful anointing, relaxed on a stool and began a playful banter with a few of his members. I wanted to get up but didn't want to step on everyone's feet again and so I turned to the lady next to me and asked if she thought he was about to dismiss. Her answer was yes but at that very minute, he stood up, became serious and said, "God is not through with this service yet." He then began to pray for a lady on the front row. When he finished praying for her and lifted his eyes, I felt he was looking my way. He then walked straight back, laid his hands on me, and began to pray. He was praying things over me that no one but God and I knew. He stopped and asked, "Have we ever met before?" Then began praying again. Suddenly his voice became strong and I felt God was speaking as he said, "God has put a conviction on you to pray, you have been praying for events and people that you don't know, and yes, God says he has put a certain amount of time in your heart to fast and pray." The voice became more powerful and stronger as he continued to minister to me.

I was still rejoicing the next day and I called the church to see if they recorded the service. The sweet lady that answered the phone said they did but their practice was to stop when the message was over and because of the long service that day that the tape would likely have run out. She was kind but didn't give me any hope. I asked if she would check anyway and was ecstatic when she called to tell me that the message to me was recorded. She sounded so happy for me and I drove there that very day to pick it up. This was so important to me because I wanted to hear every word that was spoken to me and ponder its relevance. I not only listened to the tape several times, I wrote it down word for word and laminated it. Every time I read it, I am renewed by the power and glory of God.

Roger and I never did talk to Daniel about business. Our God had other plans for the service that day. We should never question when we have a "feeling" or a "nudge" in our spirit.

When a Loving Heavenly Father Intervenes

What Happened to Me
A Quiet Resting Place
God Paid off My Car
Someone Keeps Asking the Same Question
Seriously, Did God Just Flush My Commode
Do You Drink Distilled Water?
Had I Come for Nothing
Free Conference
That's Cool

What Happened to Me
Be Angry and Sin Not

Be angry and sin not, Ephesians 4:26. Why hadn't I thought about that before? I was driving out of the parking lot of a massage therapist training office holding tightly to the steering wheel with both hands and saying aloud, "What in the H is wrong with me? I was about to let a woman that had an affair with my husband practice on me to gain her certificate in massage therapy. I must be totally crazy." I shouted to no one. Then the tears came as I drove and squeezed the wheel. I had gotten to this point after I rushed home from work and then drove forty-five minutes in traffic to accommodate her since she needed one more massage to finish her training. Then she said it was too late and she would have to do it another time. She hadn't actually asked me to do this, someone else in the family asked me and I could have said no. Why didn't I? I had spent my life never really being angry... about anything. I got hurt and then allowed myself to be hurt again and again. I allowed my children to be hurt without getting angry enough to stop it. I questioned God that day. Could I be missing one of the senses like another person might lose their sense of smell? I realized, as I cried out to God, that my perception of anger was always sin. If you were angry, you screamed and cursed and lashed out at someone. And even though God does not want us to act in that manner, neither does he want us to be mistreated, stepped upon and abused. Be angry enough to take a stand when someone wants to step over your boundaries and convince you to do something that you do not feel is right. Be angry if you are not shown respect or if trust is broken. Be angry enough to remove yourself or your children from a situation that is abusive either physically or mentally. You *can* be angry and sin not

I Was Happy Living in My Trailer A Quiet Resting Place

I was happy and peaceful living in my little trailer. It definitely was not fancy but after my younger son painted and my son-in-law and my children's father repaired the huge hole in the kitchen floor and installed the new metal cabinets from Home Depot, I decided to shop for carpet. I found a man who had nice carpet pulled out of beautiful homes that had bought new. He carpeted my whole trailer except the kitchen and bathroom for next to nothing. I tell you, *I* had some *luxurious* carpet in that little trailer home. It didn't look like much from the outside but it was cozy inside. Then my oldest son and his daddy built a car port for me. The three of them built a fairly large porch. The car port was extra wide and I was grateful to them every time it rained and I had plenty of room to open and close the umbrella when I was getting in or out of the car. It was truly amazing, the little things that made me happy. My kids complained about where I lived and could not believe I could be happy there. It was beyond their understanding that I could come from a nice two story home in a good neighborhood to *this*. By this time we had sold our retail businesses including the video stores and an advertising business I started was not going well but I was blessed that I had hardly any bills. I would buy a large bag of chips for the week and have a 99 cent whopper with water every day (remember the Burger King promotion with the whoppers), but my contentment and hap-

103

piness came from deep within. The praise and intercession that went on inside the walls of that trailer home was glorious. I realized that my children thought I was a little crazy but who could blame them. Isaiah 32: 17 and 18, "And the work of righteousness shall be peace: and the effect of righteousness, quietness and assurance for ever. And my people shall dwell in a peaceable habitation, and in sure dwellings, and in quiet resting places."

God, You're Going to Have to Get Me the Payments

I felt God wanted me to keep my car so I told him, "If you want me to keep this car, you will have to get me the payments." I was in trouble again. Most of my pay had gone to my friend and new employer to pay back for my previous month's car payment It had been getting really difficult to make a payment of $280.00 a month, while working a business that was steadily going down. I felt I needed to make some quick financial decisions as I was preparing to go in a new direction and look for some kind of work that I could do. I prayed about what to do about my car. I asked my brother his advice and help in finding an older automobile that I could purchase with the equity I had accrued in my 95 Honda Accord. My friend, upon hearing my plans, wrote a check for one month's payment. Thus began my short career in the floral business. In order to pay her back, I began work in one of her shops with very minimum wages.

For several months, before she wrote the check and I began working for her, I was having a real struggle with my tithing and giving. It was so bad that I would write a check for my tithes and then have to tear it up because I wrote the money out for another need. Everywhere I turned, I began to hear sermons on the radio and at church about tithing. I prayed and asked God to turn off the adding machine in my head (it would keep going even after I was lying in bed trying to sleep). My goal was to write a tithe check and not worry whether there was enough left to pay bills. About a month before I prayed the "God if you want me to keep this car" prayer, I was in a particularly moving service at my church, and practicing my determination for faith to trust in God for my needs, I dropped a $20.00 bill in the offering plate. This may not sound like much but it was the only cash I had at that time and I had about $10.00 in the bank. Would God think this is crazy and irresponsible, I thought, as I walked out of the service, as I now had no gas money and not even a dollar for a whopper. As I walked onto the parking lot, my pastor called me over and mentioned that he wanted to pay me for a couple of tapes that I loaned him. The tapes were purchased at a "Catch the Fire Conference" and he failed to return them week after week. The tapes had only cost a couple of dollars, so of course, I said no. As he came toward me, I backed up. In his customary humorous and charming manner, he said, "This is your pastor speaking, stop now and be still." He grabbed my hand and pressed cash into it and then he backed up from me and raised his hands as he began saying, "Thank you, Lord for letting me get that off my chest." I walked away laughing as he still had his arms in the air. My laughter turned into tears when I got to my car, opened my hand and saw *two* twenty dollar bills. I was so moved that I wrote a letter to him letting him know about the struggles I was having with giving (he had no idea) and what a wonderful God we had who used him to double my offering. I closed with how I knew now that God would take care of my needs no matter what. He greeted me after church one evening and I could see the compassion in his eyes and his demeanor as he commented that the letter had made him cry.

Now my March car payment was due. As I was leaving church after the Sunday morning service, a member of the church walked up and reached to shake my hand. He deposited a $100 bill in my hand and hastily walked off. As I was standing there marveling in this, the same thing happened again. That night in the evening service, it happened again! That Sunday, I had my car payment plus $20.00. I felt my pastor was responsible for the generosity of my fellow saints though he never admitted it and the truth is, he absolutely had no idea about my concerns with my car. I wondered what was going to happen the next month and I didn't have to wait long. A past business associate called and said, "I am going to fax you a copy of a business I have built under you." He paid for my position in a marketing company and placed distributors under me in order to excite me and get me to work the business. He said, "All you have to do is purchase a product and you will get a check for $480.00." Another car payment with money left over! For the next twenty six months I got various amounts but *never* lower than my car payment and there were months that hit over $700.00. When I paid my last car payment, the check from this company suddenly dropped to a little less than $300.00. I had a good job then so I was not surprised that within a couple of months the check had dwindled to almost nothing. I don't think I would be *crazy* at all to say that *God* paid for my car.

Someone Keeps Asking the *Same* Question

She spoke these words as she looked in my direction. There were several of us that gathered together at a friend's home to pray for a young lady that was quite ill and going through other struggles in her life. My friend invited a guest that she had become acquainted with when she attended a women's prayer retreat. She asked her new friend to let the Holy Spirit be her guide and lead us in whatever direction that she felt inspired. We gathered around praying for the young lady but because of the crowd everyone couldn't get close enough to actually lay hands on her so there were quite a few of us in the outer circles laying our hands on each other making a solid bond of prayer. I felt so guilty because I kept praying for myself. I appeared part of the unified voice and I *was* praying for her or trying to but my mind kept jumping back to my plea, "Lord, please let me know what I should do. You know I want to do the right thing. If I should go back and try again, please give me a confirmation." I blended right in according to my outward appearance. There would be no way in the natural to guess that I was not putting the same petition before God as everyone else. Suddenly the appointed leader of our gathering lifted her head, turned in my direction and without making an obvious eye contact, spoke with an exasperated and almost whining voice. "God is saying, someone keeps asking me the same question over and over. I've *already* given you the answer."(And he had, over and over again in numerous ways. Our Heavenly Father has set up rules and recommendations that if we follow we can have an abundant life but that doesn't mean he condones and is happy with suffering and sadness on our part when we have done everything we can and still have no control over the situation. A Christian minister and counselor said it best when he told me "I think God feels bad for you.") With those words, she resumed praying over the young woman. It was if there were no interruption and I doubt that anyone actually caught the message except me. I could never understand why God extended so much love and patience toward me but I knew that night that *we* can try God much in the same way as the child that insists on coming back again and again even after we have given him our best, loving and carefully considered answer especially when the answer contains the words no or do not.

Seriously, Did God Just Flush My Commode

It can't be *crazy*, I was right there and I saw it happen when *God flushed my commode*. I was so tired, both physically and mentally. My finances were still in chaos and Satan had barraged me with endless attacks of kidney and bladder infections. I would get rid of one only for it to come back again. I *knew* this was an attack against the wonderful peace and close walk that I had begun with my Lord, yet I was so exhausted that in the evening when I was cleaning and preparing to close the floral shop, I would lie down on the couch just to gain enough strength to finish. It was one of those evenings and I had arrived home anxious to shower and go to bed. I flushed my commode (which was actually a good one that I had purchased when my family was fixing up my trailer), and it *happened again*. The toilet was good but the plumbing was so old that it was a fairly common occurrence for the water to back up. This time, it came rushing over the lid and onto the floor. By the time I could squat down and reach the cut off valve, there was about an inch of dirty water all over the bathroom floor. I cleaned up the floor and plunged and plunged and nothing happened. I was afraid to turn the water back on and try to flush again. It was still at the top ready to spill out again. I was so tired, I just sat down on the floor and cried as I said these words, "God, please help me, please unstop this commode." Almost instantly, there was a loud (very loud) swoosh and I opened my eyes just in time to see the water go down. It was such a forceful, actually a *supernatural* flush, that I will never forget it.

Do You Drink Distilled Water

"Do you drink distilled water?" This question came from a lady that was leading a small prayer meeting. There were only three of us there in the little flower shop that belonged to my friend who was unable to attend, so I was praying with two women that I had not previously met. I had been going through difficult times that had stretched into years but this particular season in my life was especially challenging as physical ailments were added to the continual spiritual battles and questions that I faced. It had been less than two weeks since I stopped taking my sixth antibiotic because it was making me so ill and I was so tired of fighting. The moment I threw the medicine bottle into the trash, I cried out to God in an anguished and tormented voice, "Only you know what is wrong with me and you are the only one that can help. The doctors don't know and I sure don't know." We had been praying and worshipping for some time when the question was put forth. I was stunned when I realized she was looking at me. Before I could answer, she looked squarely at me and stated with indisputable authority, "God wants you to drink distilled water," then with a little confused hesitancy, she said, "and don't eat chocolate." She said this with more of a question in her voice as if she didn't understand it. Then she said, again with the same question in her voice, "And don't go back." I told her that maybe the distilled water was for the bladder and kidney infection I had been fighting for months and that I knew what "Don't go back" meant but had to laugh as I added that the chocolate was God's sense of humor as I have had a special love and craving for chocolate all of my life.

I bought distilled water that night and drank it exclusively for years but unfortunately I only deprived myself of chocolate for about a year. Three days later I was visiting a service at a church that advertised special speakers who were a husband and wife missionary team. When the invitation was extended to come to the altar for prayer, I came forward with expectancy and with the same request that was always with me, to hear instructions for my life. Even though my back was still in pain and I was still dealing with infection; I was drinking distilled water and felt confident that it was being taken care of. When the couple came to me in line, to my surprise, she put her hand on my back right where the pain was and as he prayed silently behind her, I heard these words, "God is washing that infection right out of your body," and then they moved on. *How could anyone, anywhere deny the greatness of our God.*

Had I Come for Nothing

I was so tired. My emotions, brain, mind, and body felt drained. Yet I was here. I had driven four hours by myself after a friend had to cancel. I finished registration and walked into the service late. It was an extremely anointed service with the Spirit of God moving through the auditorium, just what I yearned for, yet I sat there, unmoved, while others basked in the glory of God. As I walked out, early, the praise and worship was ringing in my ears. What is wrong with me, I cried out to God, as I walked with head down to my hotel room. I had anticipated this conference for months and though I couldn't really afford it, I booked everything including a nice room in the same hotel on a credit card. My plan was to read the word and pray, to seek direction for the service in the morning, yet I crawled into bed with these words to God. "I am so sorry, I will get up early to pray before the morning session." I was truly sad and disgusted with myself.

I awoke with a start and jumped out of bed when I realized I had less than an hour to get dressed and make the first service on time. I felt better but was very upset that I was not going to have time for extended prayer. I talked to God as I rushed around getting ready to leave. Just as I was walking out of the door, the Spirit of God gave that little nudge that I had felt a couple of times before, that I should open the word. My mind said, "It's too late, I've got to leave" but my Spirit man insisted so I let the door go, stepped back into the room and opened my Bible.

My eyes fell upon Isaiah 6:8, *"Also I heard the voice of the Lord, saying, Whom shall I send, and who will go for us? Then said I, Here am I; send me."* I read a little more of the passage and then ran out. My thoughts were that at least I could be on time for service. The praise and worship was awesome but I was still lost in my feelings of unworthiness. Then the first speaker came to the floor and the first words out of his mouth were from the very scripture I had just read. I thought my heart would burst with love for my Savior. Of course I examined in my heart all the reasons for that word given to me and how that I might be able to fulfill the scripture but one thing is for certain, my loving God let me know that he was with me, was aware of me and still ready when I would seek him with my whole heart.

Free Conference

I have attended several Benny Hinn Conferences but now he was promoting a free conference, the only one that I have heard about before or since. Crusades, yes but not free conferences. It was only a four hour drive away from my home so an acquaintance and I decided to attend and to make it even more cost effective we spent the night with a friend of mine that lived in the same city.

All went well until we got to the conference. The crowds were overwhelming and the lines were long. We were fortunate that we arrived early enough that we only had about a two hour wait in line yet there were those that had been in line far longer than us. We knew they would be sending overflow crowds to other parts of the facility to view on a big screen and my traveling buddy was steadily grumbling that she wasn't about to partake of the service by watching it on a screen after traveling all of that way. To make matters worse, the heat was unbearable to me and I was weak and nauseated. We were so happy when we barely made it in the door and were shown a couple of seats in an already overcrowded auditorium. A few minutes after we were seated, an usher asked my friend to move to a row right in front in order to let a parent sit with his child that was already seated. She displayed such anger that I was embarrassed for her. She refused to move saying she was sitting there by her friend (me). I felt so bad that I ignored her ranting and volunteered to move. Of course, she immediately realized that she had been unreasonable and was somewhat sorry but was still very unhappy. I, on the other hand, was delighted to be there sitting and waiting. I started a conversation with the lady on my left. I listened intently and with delight as she related such interesting life experiences. She was in show business and had worked in film as an actress as well as in production. She related how she had moved away from the spotlight in order to pursue Jesus. She was beautiful, smart, and well-spoken and was actually doing *something*. We hit it off and even though I envied her walk with God, I liked her very much.

On the drive home, I had time to think of the conversation and felt so let down that I was not where I should be. I felt all of *the emotions* that have always plagued me. I am not close enough, obedient enough or spiritual enough to deserve the favor of my Father in heaven.

A few days after I arrived home, I received a surprise package in the mail. It was sent to me by my newly found "angel," a book by Joyce Meyer entitled *When, God, When?* A teaching on God's timing for our lives as well as a video entitled *The Silent Years*, also by Joyce Meyer. I don't remember giving her my address but I am so grateful for her obedience to the Spirit of God. She actually stated in a note to me, "The Holy Spirit wanted me to send you these materials."

Zech. 4:6, "Not by might nor by power but by my spirit, saith the Lord."

That's Cool

She had a look on her face that suggested that I had lost it and then she blurted out with her childlike contagious laugh, "That's cool, you mean I was used by God." My friend was a business acquaintance that was known for being completely light hearted, not a serious bone in her body. She told everyone that her husband and she had made a pact to make everything fun. On this day we had sat together at a chamber networking luncheon and were preparing to leave. The morning had not gone well for me. About an hour before the event, I was still at home and got a call from my friend whom was compensating me for the help I gave her in her business. In fact, I had helped her a lot and the event I was getting ready for was to promote her flower shop with no monetary reward. She jumped all over me about some information she received from someone who worked for her. She accused me of wanting to hurt another person, of being untruthful, and in general made me feel very unworthy. In the vulnerable state of mind I was in, I wondered if it could be true. I knew that this individual was very dramatic and was always in some sort of conflict with one person or another but since she was a practicing Christian, I was very hurt. I had been seeking God during that time in my life and had begun to feel very close to what he desired of me. I began to weep and continued to do so while driving to the luncheon. I told God that if it were true to please reveal it to me. The luncheon took my mind off my problems and I truly enjoyed myself as I interacted with other business owners. There was no earthly reason for Kathy to walk up to me and say, "You are the sweetest person, so kind and caring and I can't imagine you ever wanting to hurt another person." My eyes filled with tears and even though I didn't know anything about her spiritual condition, I told her that I had just prayed for God to let me know if he was disappointed with me. She seemed so genuinely happy to know that she helped. God can use anyone, any time. He is a great and merciful God.

Praise God, It's Going to Be All Right

It's Been Two Weeks
I Will Lift Mine Eyes unto the Hills
He Stood There with Paint in His Hair
I'm Really Writing
We Really Can Ask for Favor
It's Not You, Reba
Taking Audrey to the Movies

It's Been Two Weeks Today

As I was about to leave for work at my friend's floral shop, I remembered that it had been exactly two weeks to the day since I prayed for God's guidance on whether it was time to leave my current employment and had set the time frame for two weeks.

When I first began to work for her, I was so grateful for kindnesses that she extended above and beyond the car payment that she made for me that I went out of my way to repay her. I attended networking events on my days off to promote her business. Initially, I was in charge of one of her shops and I was the only one there so I treated it like my own. All of the large floral work was done at the main location so I only took orders, sold completed pieces out of the cooler or did minor adjustments and of course kept the place clean. I enjoyed the freedom and the flexibility but then her husband decided that he wanted me to work at the main shop. Soon after, they became extremely critical, and in my opinion, unfair. They both, and especially her, had a reputation for being controlling and petty but I had only observed it and had not been the object of any ill treatment until very recently. I battled with my unhappiness and each time that I would think of leaving, I would tell myself that I was being taught to be humble. I observed their non-Christian attitude toward others but also observed genuine love and concern, as well.

So it was with a torn heart that I prayed for God to give me a sign on what I should do as I reminded him that I still needed to make a living. The last two weeks had gone so well that it was a wonder that I was even reminded that it had been two weeks since I prayed for an answer. I had barely been at work when I was called to the back to be reprimanded for something so trivial that I can't even remember what it was. It was so unnecessary that I couldn't believe that it was happening. At that moment, I made my decision to leave and felt total peace. I confided in a wonderful Christian woman that ran a home for unwed mothers who was in the shop that day volunteering her time to unravel some mistakes that had been made in their financial records. Even though she applauded my decision, her first reaction was to warn me that this would be taken as a personal betrayal and I would not be treated well. I prayed for the right words to say and I was astonished when she looked at me with a sweet expression and seemed to accept my words as if God had confirmed my decision. Almost immediately, I got a call from the editor of the local paper who asked me if I would be interested in doing some contract work. I would be neither employed by the chamber of commerce nor the newspaper but would sell ads that would pay for the cost of a chamber publication that would be inserted into the newspaper. It would only pay about a $100 for the month but I said yes and I knew immediately that God was giving me the assurance that he was going to provide. Within a week, I had a call from another friend that offered me a temporary position to set up an office and market for them. I cannot express the love I feel for the Holy Spirit as he speaks to us and guides us when we will listen to his voice.

I Will Lift Mine Eyes
unto the Hills

The pages opened and my eyes fell on this passage. Psalm 121: *"I will lift up mine eyes unto the hills, from whence cometh my help. My help cometh from the Lord, which made heaven and earth. He will not suffer thy foot to be moved: he that keepeth thee will not slumber. Behold, he that keepeth Israel shall neither slumber nor sleep. The Lord is thy keeper: the Lord is thy shade upon thy right hand. The sun shall not smite thee by day, nor the moon by night. The Lord shall preserve thee from all evil: he shall preserve thy soul. The Lord shall preserve thy going out and thy coming in from this time forth, and even forever more."*

My ongoing spiritual struggles ran parallel to my seemingly unending financial situation. When my network marketing business failed, I sold jewelry that I had left over and even pawned some of it. I was still eating the dollar whoppers and checking on my mom a *lot*. Mom always had something cooked. Then God provided me the job with my friend that owned the two florist shops. God provided again, and now my three month stint for another friend to set up an internet business was ending. I knew the job was temporary but I was confident that I was going to be taken care of. My assignment was to market it, set up the web site and have it running smoothly. Clark paid me what I had agreed upon that would just get me by. I was still selling ads (contract) for the Chamber publication which even though it only netted me about $100.00 a month, it afforded me the opportunity to do something that I thoroughly enjoyed and that was to write articles for a different spotlighted business each month. Then I got a call from the publisher who had given me this opportunity. He said there was a new classified department being set up in one of their locations that was about an hour's drive from my home. I called to set up an interview. As I was preparing to leave, the morning of the interview, I had one of those moments; when you look at the Bible and you *know* God wants to tell you something. *Not* picking up your Bible and praying, "God, give me a word" and then opening at random to a page, but when you *know*. I had reached the door when I turned around and went back to open the word. Even now, I can feel the excitement that I felt that day. I knew My God was going to take care of me. On the drive to the interview, I changed the *thees* and *thys* to *me* and *my* and said the passage over and over. I had it memorized when I arrived. For weeks, I recited that passage on the way to work at my new job and on the way home.

He Stood There with Paint in His Hair

I jerked the car quickly into the convenience store gas bar and hurriedly jumped out. As I ran in, I glanced at the man standing by the checkout counter. He had a pleasant smile but what I noticed the most was that his hair was sticking up all over with paint in it. I was in a hurry because I had taken the morning off to interview for a position that would put me closer to home and very close to my mother. I told God how much that I appreciated the job that he had given me but that it sure would be nice to be in a place where I would be able to check on her and drop by at lunchtime, so it was no surprise to me when I learned that a position was available that would answer my prayer. The interview had gone well and I was told that I would have a yes or no answer by the end of the week after all the interviews were finished. I planned to work through lunch thus the quick stop for some crackers and a coke. As I hurriedly stepped up to the checkout, the man was still smiling as he waved me on ahead of him. I protested but he assured me with a smile and a wave that he was in no hurry. I smiled back and thanked him. I grabbed my stuff and thanked him again as I rushed out. My car was parked right by the door almost blocking it and as I reached for the handle to get in, I realized the man with paint all over him was standing in the door of the store. It was obvious to assume that he was a painter that had taken a break from his work. As I looked back at his still smiling face, he asked, "Are you a minister?" I laughed as I recalled when Clarence had said the very same thing and I answered no, then I was admonished and given a lesson on how we are all ministers, so I said, "If you are asking if I pastor or preach, the answer is no." He stepped closer and I realized this was going to be one of those "Heavenly Moments." He explained that he felt that I was a minister because of the message he was hearing from God and then asked if I minded if he related a "word" from God meant for me. I was stunned as he began to tell me that there was going to be a change that was starting that day. He said he felt God was telling him that I was starting a new ministry and felt that strongly, but hesitantly said maybe it meant a career change. We talked for a few moments. He said he was a minister but he didn't have a card. I asked where he preached. He gave me a vague answer and all I remember was that it was not in that area. I gave him my card, thanked him and left. I was excited as I got back on the road heading for work knowing that I was going to get the position that I wanted. When I sat down at my desk, the first thing I did was to listen to my messages. I was not surprised when I heard the voice of the president of the chamber saying, "I've canceled the other interviews so if you still want to work here, the position is yours."

When I was going home that evening on the road that I had traveled over so many times, I realized that I didn't know which store I had been in that morning. There were only three gas bars on that forty-mile stretch of mostly nothing with two of them on the side of the road that I stopped, but neither one looked right. And what about that nice smiling man with the pleasant face. What was he doing there since he told me that he didn't live or preach in the area. I can still see him and I will always wonder if God put him there just for me. I love my Heavenly Father.

I'm Really Writing

My job description at the chamber of commerce does not list writing but I am making reports on chamber committees that I choose to make interesting and descriptive. I am writing letters that are not required of me, to chamber members, thanking them for their involvement whether it is a time commitment or a financial one. I am eagerly volunteering to write articles for our chamber publication, especially the events that I am involved with such as the monthly luncheons. It is so gratifying that I don't mind the extra time and hours that I put in. I recently had a chance to write an article for the local newspaper and was paid $25.00. Someone might think I had been paid $1,000 if you gauged it by my excitement. I still desire to make a differ-ence in whatever world that I find myself in. The job at the chamber has truly expanded my territories (1 Chronicles 4:10). I have met so many wonderful God loving people and I feel so blessed that we now say a prayer before each of our various committee meetings. I take great pride in selecting and seeking ministers of the Gospel to lead the prayer at our monthly luncheons. We now have two ministers on the board of directors at the chamber. I am totally committed and loyal to this organization. My sister-in-law recently announced, with confidence and pride and in her most excited elevated voice. "You have a ministry at the chamber." My pastor told me about meeting with a chamber member about local business and my name came up in conversation. He proudly proclaimed, "You are a great ambassador for the kingdom"

I am beginning to relax and think one of my pastor friends may be right on target when he says that I have a ministry at the chamber. I so hope my God is at least partially pleased with me and I do love my job.

We Really Can Ask God for Favor?

I find myself remembering supernatural favor that I have received. I have been resting on past favors from God and flying high on the respect and mutual endearment that I enjoy with those that I work for and with. It didn't come from my merits. When I first began the work that I do now, I was intimidated and got off to a bad start with a malicious coworker. She was out to get anyone she could and succeeded in causing some to leave either through being asked to do so or becoming so discouraged that they gave up. She was so talented in her "evil" ways that she was able to influence those in higher positions and cause them to see and believe things that were not true. I was praying with a friend, one that I had worked with and for on various projects, and I shared my feelings. She was fairly new to the kind of worship and Spirit walk that I enjoyed yet sometimes she amazed me with her childlike faith. She began to pray earnestly and fervently for favor in my current situation. Someone had told her she could do that and she accepted it. I am ashamed to say that I had never prayed for favor in that way and most of the time I felt superior to her in my knowledge of Spiritual ways. I am not proud of the condescending attitude that I have displayed in the past so I listened to her prayer and wondered if we could really expect an answer. It is almost unbelievable how things unfolded. Notes from business owners began to come into the office praising me for my projects and ethics. Suddenly the trouble maker became the one in trouble and was asked to leave. Everything was in a kind of chaos and I could see the beginning of a change in attitude toward me. Then God sent in a whirlwind. A marketing person for a new company began to befriend me. She was well liked and respected and although she didn't know why, she began to brag about everything I did. Unusual things happened, like the time we were in a board meeting and she began to give me credit for "just doing my job" Before it was over, everyone from CEO's to small business owners were clapping for me. I saw some of their faces with the "deer in the headlights" look and I had to laugh to myself knowing they had no idea that they were part of a "God thing"... supernatural favor. The precious lady that prayed for me is no longer living on this earth and though I have some unfavorable memories of her, I can never forget her for praying for "favor" for me. It is a lasting legacy of hers and it goes on in my prayers for myself and my family. Thank you, Lord, for loving us and bestowing unmerited favor when we ask.

It's Not You, Reba

"It's not you, Reba," I uttered, "It's God." With that, I hung up the phone, turned to my computer and started typing a prayer. I received a call a few minutes earlier from the president of a professional organization that I was a member of, asking me to say the invocation at the meeting that day. When I hesitated, she explained that it was okay, "I'll be able to get someone else," she said. As soon as I hung up the phone, I felt the guilt. I had just returned, two days earlier, from a prayer conference where hands were laid on me to receive an anointing for prayer and yet I hesitated and flinched when God gave me the opportunity to pray with anointment. What was wrong with me? I called her back and said I would. She replied that she was sorry and didn't mean to put pressure on me. That's when I told her that it wasn't her applying the pressure. The prayer God gave me was beautiful and meaningful. I was still anxious, (very nervous) but when I finished, I heard several amens. I sat back down at my place and my body tightened up and went into something that seemed like a seizure. I couldn't breathe, I couldn't talk, and my whole body was in a lock down mode that was extremely painful. As I muttered in my mind, "God, you can't let me die now" the pain subsided and I could breath. What a scary moment and all because I just said a prayer to the one I love so much and said it where others could hear. I'm sure that would be one of the times that he thought I was crazy. Can't you just hear him chuckle and imagine his reaction! I love him.

Taking Audrey to the Movies

I took a day off during the week for some week end work and I had an urge to pick my friend Audrey up and take her to the movies. She is ten years older than me, in fairly good health and still drives herself pretty much where she wants to go. I didn't feel spiritual about it at all, just the nagging desire to pick her up and spend the day. She lives quite a ways from me so we don't see each other often and our conversations on the phone are rare. I enlisted another longtime friend, that is my age and who had only met Audrey once or twice over a thirty-year period, to go with me. Judy drove an hour from the west side of town to meet me in the northeast and then we proceeded together to drive south for another forty-five minutes to pick her up. When it comes to movies, I don't care for musicals. I knew Judy did and when she suggested it, I was prepared to shoot it down but then Audrey said in her sweet, precious voice, "Oh, I love musicals." I was surprised that she was so quick to express that because I knew she had not attended a movie in years. The movie was great and to my surprise, I actually enjoyed it. We had a lovely day. There was lunch before the movie and dinner afterward with a stop at a little tearoom in between. At the end of the day after Judy was safely deposited at her vehicle and I was driving Audrey home, she began to tell me how much the day had meant to her. She had been dealing with issues concerning her granddaughter. She related to me how much stress she had been under and all the prayers and tears that had gone up for her family. I hadn't had a clue of what she was going through and although I was ashamed that I hadn't kept in closer touch, I was amazed and pleased at how we can be used in such simple ways as taking a friend to the movies.

God's Unending Mercies

I Come to the Garden Alone

I began to sing in her ear, the old song "I Come to the Garden Alone while the dew is still on the roses." She squeezed my hand and I continued to love on her and talk to her. I didn't know why I was singing that particular song as I had not heard the tune in years, let alone sung it.

You can never be ready to lose a parent but I realized that it should be much easier on me, at my age, than if I had been thirty or even forty years old. In February, 2003, I took my mom to the doctor for a routine checkup. Upon noticing the blue hue in her fingertips, he ordered a chest X-ray. He called me into another room and his exact words were "The Party's Over." This was my beloved mother and that is all that he said. My two brothers and I went to great lengths in prolonging the news of the diagnosis even though we knew that it was inevitable. We enlisted the doctor's help and arranged delayed tests and appointments. She and I took a trip to Dallas, one that had been planned already, to visit her granddaughter who was attending college and also visit a favorite niece who lived on the outskirts of the city. We had a great time. After she was told the complete diagnosis, we still did little things, a trip to New Braunfels, a trip to a bed and breakfast, and though she rarely went to the movies, she asked me to take her. I chose a comedy and delighted in her laughter. We went to church on Mother's Day with many family members in attendance. Her strength held up until the end of May and she was able to attend my younger brother's graduation (he went back to school to get a degree in education). I hung on to the words spoken by the oncologist, "six months or so." I still had a few things I wanted to do with her. We talked about some of them. Then she was diagnosed by the hospice nurse with a kidney infection. She was a sweet and kind young caretaker but did not give her a strong enough antibiotic. I demanded a stronger one. I forgot the purpose of hospice which is not to prolong life if it involves suffering. I still thought she would get over the infection and we would have some more time. She got a little better each day but after three weeks she still could not get out of the chair or bed by herself. Her strength was gone. One of my brothers would come over in the morning and one at night to help me with her. One Monday evening after work, I sat by her chair and we talked about the next day and what we planned to do. She was so weak and when my baby brother came over, he commented on it. She went to sleep that night and never woke up again. From Tuesday morning until the following Saturday night, we kept a vigil by her side. Grandkids, friends, and neighbors came and went but my brothers and their wives were there with me. One night, about 2:00 a.m., I found that one brother and his wife had gone home to rest and change and my other brother was asleep on a chair. This was my chance to talk to her alone. I was not ready for her to go and I told God so. I needed more time. It was not going as I had thought and it was hard for me to accept. I had the feeling that I should have done more and maybe she felt that way too. Although she never responded, she was constantly talked to and sung to by family members. I did not join in the singing because I can't carry a tune. On this night, I got her hand and sobbed, "Mom, please if you hear me and love me just squeeze my hand," as I began singing to her.

It had been two days since the funeral, everyone was gone and I was home alone. I was devastated, my cries were like deep groans, and suddenly I heard a new song on our local Christian radio station. It was a slightly updated beautiful rendering of "I Come to the

Garden Alone." Immediately, I knew God was letting me know that he knew my pain. I heard this song continuously after that because my radio at home, work and in the car was tuned in to this Christian station. A couple of months later I was in Gruene, Texas. I was thinking of Mom and walked into a shop that was playing this very hymn. I couldn't see where it was coming from, so I asked the clerk. She said it was from a CD by Elvis Presley. I bought it, of course. The funny thing is that no matter where the CD was when I stopped the car, it always started with that song. Never mind that my other CDs would begin where it left off. My son said that I must be doing something differently. Maybe my son doesn't know my God the way I do but then maybe *he* thinks I'm crazy, too.

God Is Wrapping Her in a Pretty Package

My daughter looked intently at my three-year-old granddaughter and began to speak, "Jesus is going to wrap me-ma in a pretty box so we can see her before she leaves with him." She knew she would have to prepare the baby for what she would see when they arrived to view the body of my mother the afternoon before the services. She barely got the words out before the protest began. "No, she is not in a box, don't cry, Mama, she is with Jesus." My daughter was speechless when her little girl's small arms wrapped around her as she began to comfort her mother. Later, she called me and asked, "Have you already prepared her for the funeral and Grandma's passing?" I had not.

My granddaughter and my mom had a special bond. It was so unique that my daughter and I marveled at the change that occurred in such a hyper child when she was around her MeMa. The mutual love affair started before she was two years old. She drove her mother crazy wanting to go see MiMi and MeMa. When she had my attention, it was go, go, go, do this and do that, but the minute she was in the presence of MeMa, she would be content to "read" her a story or even allow MeMa to read one. She would sit in Mom's chair with her for an extended length of time. A small miracle. When Mom got really sick and was in her last months, she could no longer get out of her chair. We had to move her from bed to wheelchair and then to her comfortable chair. The baby would sit on the arm of the chair, holding her book and "reading," even when her MeMa was sound asleep. They would share meals and snacks together on a TV tray. It was truly amazing. The last week of her life when Mom slipped into a coma and was confined to a hospital bed in her bedroom, we thought it unusual that it was so easy to keep the baby out of the bedroom even though she knew her MeMa was in there. It was like she *knew,* for which we were grateful to not have to talk about it. The morning my mother died, the baby was kept away until the body was taken out of the house and then, of course, family stayed with me all day. My daughter thought it strange that a child that once seemingly lived to visit with her MeMa didn't ask about her and not once ventured into the bedroom. In fact, she happily visited with other family members and played outside on the swing set. My daughter whispered to me that she would have to tell her but would delay until the last possible minute.

The scene at the funeral home was unforgettable. My daughter stood at the casket, holding *her* daughter, and cried. My granddaughter did not look at the casket. Her eyes were focused on her mother's face. She took her little hands and tried to wipe away the tears as she said, "Don't cry, Mommy, MeMa is not here, she is dancing with Jesus." While I was trying to erase my doubts and have faith that my mom was truly happy and in heaven, my granddaughter had a direct line to Jesus.

"Clarence... Again?"

Could this be Clarence, I thought, as he grabbed my hand to pray for me. I was standing in a store that had seemingly appeared out of nowhere with an apparent stranger that wanted to pray for me.

It had been two weeks since I lost my mother. I was back at work and was on my way down Main Street in our tiny, history rich town to deliver some materials to a chamber member when I noticed a business on my left, in a fairly run down section of old buildings, that had not been there a day or two before. My job with the chamber of commerce, among other things, entailed welcoming new businesses to the community so I knew that I would be stopping there on my way back. All of a sudden, the traffic cleared and before I knew what I was doing, I made a left turn into a drive of an old house renovated into a florist shop. I turned around and headed back to the new business, all the time wondering why I made that decision. I walked into the store and there stood a well-dressed black gentleman talking to the store's owner. I was patiently waiting when the owner paused and turned to me, signaling that I could take a turn. I introduced myself to him with a welcome from the chamber. Upon hearing that, the man who had paused his conversation for me, exclaimed, "Well this must be a divine appointment. We need to talk." At that moment, a young lady walked into the business. She was from the local newspaper. We started chatting, and something (I don't remember what) led to the fact that she attended the church that my mother was a member of and her mother helped with the food for my family the day of the funeral. Then, I felt a warm and comforting hand take mine and a gentle voice said, "This *is* a divine appointment," and began praying for me to let go of my "Unnatural Grief." When he finished praying, I asked if his name was Clarence. When he said yes, I asked him if he still hung around at the Good Will Store. He laughed, and although it been seven or eight years and I had not worked for the chamber at our first meeting, he said, " I remember meeting you there and you were buying clothes for the orphans." We visited for a few more minutes and he gave me another card. He said he was pastoring a church near the area we were in. I cannot believe that I do not know where that card is and we never did get together about the chamber. With absolute surety, I can say that God does have everything under control.

God, I Can't Worry About This Now

Everyone was gone and I was alone as I quietly cried, "God, I can't worry about this now, I don't know what to do, so if I need this surgery, just work it out and I will accept your will and if it doesn't work out, then I'll just go back to work and trust you to take care of me." I was lying in a hospital bed in August of 2006. I was in such a state of confusion, uncertainty, and disbelief, not to mention being drugged, that I hadn't talked to my best friend much. After that I went to sleep and had total peace. Just four days earlier, I finished a fairly normal day at the office, only to comment to a coworker that I was either awfully tired or awfully old. At home, I began to feel dizzy and when I tried to walk, the floor was coming toward me. If this had occurred ten years prior, I would have gone to bed to sleep it off. But I was older and wiser and knew that I had some of the symptoms of a stroke. At the emergency room, the doctor said it was a TIA (Transient Ischemic Attack) and that I could probably go home soon. But then he called my doctor who wanted to admit me. Early Tuesday morning I called my office to say that I was in the hospital and not to worry, that it was not a stroke and I would see everyone the next day. But now, I had doctors coming in and out of my room, a cardiology team, an infectious disease specialist, and a neurologist. My wonderful family doctor wanted to find out what had happened. By now they knew I had a stroke at the base of my brain (a mild one) caused by a blood clot. Tests had confirmed some kind of mass in one of my heart valves, but what, thus the infectious disease specialist and the cardiologists. The miracle was that the cardiology team, a well-known and well respected group of doctors that practice not only in the local hospitals but in the Medical Center downtown, knew that I did not have insurance, yet they worked tirelessly on my case. They performed tests, visited me and called me. They felt that I needed open heart surgery at a larger hospital in the downtown Medical Center, yet that hospital didn't want to accept me. A week after my admittance and a couple of days after I turned the situation over to God, my family doctor walked in the room and the grave and somber look on his face was replaced by a big smile. He said, "We have a plan," and he began to tell me about the well-known "famous" surgeon that had agreed to perform my surgery. He had printed out information about the surgeon from a web site "for my family," he said. Three days later, a total of ten days now, I was still in the local hospital and one of the cardiologists came in. He was *so* cute as he told me how he had been down on his knees to the surgeon and the operating room was scheduled for the next morning. The problem was that the hospital still did not want to accept me. That night an ambulance was summoned and by 10:00 p.m., I was in a bed in the right place with surgery scheduled for the next morning. I have personal knowledge that my long-time family doctor and his wife are Christians, but whatever the status of the other doctors, I know that my *God* made *angels* of them to perform his good and perfect will.

The Bracelet

I was at my office going through some business cards and attempting to get organized. I picked up a card that was entitled "Circle of Friends." As I read these words, "through life's ups and downs, God blesses us with special friends to pray with us, cry with us, laugh with us and encourage us and I thank God for you, my friend." This card has been on my desk for three or four months now. I remember the day my friend rushed in, during the Christmas holidays, with a package of silver bracelets. She is always in a hurry just as I am. Unlike me, she is also a dynamic person, a born leader, who came into the chamber community like a storm and was asked to serve on the board of directors within a year and is now on the executive board. I love her dearly, everyone does, and the two of us seem like an unlikely team. In her usual manner, she hurriedly explained that I should pick one of the bracelets and that she couldn't put hers on until I had mine on my wrist. There was one with a heart and one with a cross. I decided on the one with the heart and placed it on as she watched. She explained that we should always wear them to cement our bond of friendship. She gave me the card and I hurriedly glanced at it and placed it on my desk among a few thousand other cards and other stuff. This incident was about four months after I had been in the hospital for over two weeks for the mild stroke that resulted in open heart surgery to remove a growth from a valve in my heart. I was overwhelmed with flowers, cards, calls, and visits from chamber members and friends. I had reports like "I was going to place you on the prayer list at my church but you were already on it." My boss, president of the chamber, took the time that he would ordinarily use to speak at a networking luncheon and led prayer for me. There were numerous members who donated a percentage of their business sales to a medical fund that had been set up for me. One "special hero" to me was a beautiful Christian man who organized a golf benefit that raised $10,000. There were other wonderful stories but the impact that my friend, the one who presented me with the bracelet, had on me and my family was enormous. She took time out of her busy schedule to come every day, even when I was downtown in the medical center. Sometimes she was there two or three times in a day. She was there on the morning of my surgery and she was there that evening. "She became like a member of the family" was the report that I got. I heard she was there at the times I don't remember, but I do *have* memories, such as the time she came bouncing into my hospital room with her usual jauntiness and my son promptly told her I wouldn't eat. She got a straw and, believe me, I did suck some of that soup down. You just *don't* say no to her. One thing I definitely remember was that every day that she came, she had presents. Presents that were beautifully wrapped with expensive pajamas, perfumes, lotions, beautiful sentiments, and more were presented to me and even though I can't remember the days and the times and everything that I received, I remember the beautiful smiles, and the tender warmth that came in with her. I knew we had a bond in our working relationship. She always proclaimed how she couldn't have chaired a committee without my support. She is an only child and I have no sisters so we proclaimed that we were sisters. We exchanged sarcastic barbs and tried to outdo each other in our "over the hill" birthday presents to each other. To me, she was the greatest, and I felt honored to have her as a friend but I never expected *this*. The first week I was home from the hospital, she came to my home, and brought more gifts. I protested, "I don't deserve all this." She looked at me and with our usual banter, she said, "I *know* you don't," but then she stuck her tongue out of the corner of

152

her mouth with one of her cute little expressions, pointed to the ceiling and said, "*He* made me do it." I wonder if she realized, at that moment, just how true that might have been. I wanted to do something special for her at Christmas, so my daughter helped me make a basket for her. It was big and beautiful. It had some very nice things in it as well as snacks and fun things. She told me that she cried when she found the tiny Christmas ornament that had her name as well as her four son's names imprinted on it. She lost her oldest son when he was in his twenties. The basket was nice, and she seemed genuinely pleased, but I knew that I had not come close to the wonderful gift of friendship she had given me. When we are together, we do not talk about heavenly things and get into discussions about God and church as I seem to do with everyone else I have contact with. My friend has ties to a particular religion from her childhood days and attends services occasionally. I know that she does not experience the spiritual walk that some of us are so accustomed to, and yet, what if her passion and intensity were turned toward God. This thought occurred to me as I read the card that came with the bracelet that I now have on my wrist. These words "God blesses us with special friends to pray with us" are ringing in my ears. I have recently read a book about fasting and prayer that is revitalizing my prayer life. My prayer now, is: "Please, dear Lord, don't let me fail in this assignment." If I fast and pray for my dear friend, that will be the greatest gift I can give her.

God, So Sorry for My Failures

I was at it again, I felt so inadequate about my life and what I did with it, so unworthy when I look at all of the great ministries and self-sacrificing people in this world that have made such a difference. My feelings were at one of my all-time lows when I was mindlessly scrolling down my face book page and there, written just minutes before, was a tribute by one of my grandsons. He quoted scripture and words from a gospel song and then compared it to me. "Just like when we were little, your guidance, love, and Christian witness were an inspiration to all of us." I then reached for two greeting cards that had been given to me by another of my grandsons just a few weeks before, one for my birthday and one for Mother's Day. I had tucked them away in my desk drawer because they were so precious to me. I cried when I read them. One card read "Knowing the person you are and seeing the way you live inspires us to be proud of who we are and to give our best" and then in his own words, "MiMi, you always put the needs of others in front of your own." Crying again, I picked up the birthday card and read its beautiful verse but the precious words in his own handwriting, "You are a blessing to everyone who knows you. I love you," made me realize, once again, that God is always working in our lives, doing good, if we allow him to direct our path. If that weren't enough to totally lift my Spirits, that evening my ten-year-old grandson, the baby, was complaining about his parents and some of their friends. He was so cute and sweet as he was warning me that he felt the friends were a bad influence on his mama and daddy. He proceeded to tell me that this couple said bad words and smoked cigarettes and that I needed to talk to my daughter. He ended this tirade with "I am going to grow up and be a good daddy and be a church person just like you." What a sweet blessing to have grandchildren.

Living Life

I am still just living my life. Family and work take up the largest percentage of it, yet I still yearn for that special fellowship with God that I am always striving for but falling short. My church has no Sunday night services and one Sunday, I felt the need to connect so I attended a service whose pastor I met through my chamber affiliation. My heart was immediately pricked when the topic of the sermon was announced, "Whom shall I send." My thoughts went back fifteen years to the night when God rescued my discouraged heart with those words. If that were not enough, the pastor then went into a lengthy discussion of seeking God and pronounced to the congregation that if "you will seek God with all of your heart, he will reveal himself to you." Have I done that? Have I sought God with all of my heart? The answer could be "no" because I haven't fully sacrificed my life and my time to seek him to *my* satisfaction since that was prophesized to me so many years ago. But the answer could also be "yes" because my heart is always yearning for him even in my failures. I strive to listen to his voice through the Holy Spirit and I do love him with all of my heart.

Our Lord and Savior wants us to be ready to witness whether it is a friend, or a stranger on the other side of the world. Most of us are not called to travel into unfamiliar countries to preach but we can give to those that do. Isaiah 52:7 says, *"How beautiful upon the mountains are the feet of him that bringeth good tidings."* Our God loves for us to seek his presence every day and we can do that during our very worst times as well as on our best and happiest days.

Whom shall he send? All of us. Will he reveal himself to us if we seek him? Yes, yes, and yes.

The Ending (Sort Of)

Are We There Yet?

Are We There Yet?

I've heard this question many times when traveling with my children and grandchildren and experienced their joy when we finally arrived at our destination.

I've gone through many roadblocks and numerous unnecessary detours on my life's journey. Other than our final destination that is guaranteed to be full of unimaginable glory, I so want to arrive fully intact and filled with joy in this earthly trip that I'm on, but how will I know if I'm there yet? After prolonged detours with some periods of traveling down the right roads, I have never achieved, never arrived, and never had the satisfaction of feeling that I was in God's perfect will. There were some wonderful side roads that offered temporary respite, only to lead back into the detours again.

In the last twenty years, I have been told that I have a ministry, more than once, but I never feel qualified or good enough. The truth is that I don't do enough, I do not witness effectively to the very friends that God has given to me. I pray that they see Christ in me and their actions and words tell me they do but I know that I am still failing them.

I have been able to use my time with the chamber of commerce to write articles for the business community and to live my testimony. God answered my "prayer of Jabez" and enlarged my territory and expanded the borders of a normally shy and introverted person. I have made many good friends and have numerous contacts which I have used to my advantage. I had the opportunity to write for the local newspaper. I started a new publication for the area that I live in. The magazine is family friendly and it affords me the opportunity to print scripture on the website and in the magazine as well. But I still have the driving need to be a published author. I still want to use my God given artistic talent to develop the idea that was spoken by the Spirit to my heart years ago for Christian greeting cards. I am running out of time and feel the desperate need to accomplish my desires, to "arrive." So I am wondering, when I do all of these things, will I be there yet? Or maybe we will not truly arrive until we see God in all of his Glory. Maybe, when Jesus takes me by the hand, he will say, "You have traveled a long journey, but you are here now, my child, the trip is over, you have arrived at your destination."

CPSIA information can be obtained
at www.ICGtesting.com
Printed in the USA
FFHW020723170319
51093831-56521FF